Student Interactive

Glenview, Illinois Boston, Massachusetts
Chandler, Arizona New York, New York

Pearson Education, Inc. 330 Hudson Street, New York, NY 10013

Photography

Cover: Richard Peterson/Shutterstock; Angelo Gilardelli/Shutterstock; Daniel Prudek/Shutterstock; Nick Biebach/123RF; Anatoly Tiplyashin/Shutterstock; Karina Bakalyan/Shutterstock; Eric Isselee/Shutterstock; La Gorda/Shutterstock; Cienpies Design/Shutterstock; Carolina K. Smith MD/Shutterstock; Alex Mit/Shutterstock; Aphelleon/Shutterstock; Maks Narodenko/Shutterstock

Attributions of third-party interior content appear on pages 244–245, which constitutes an extension of this copyright page.

ISBN-13: 978-0-134-90874-8
ISBN-10: 0-134-90874-0
3 19

Julie Coiro, Ph.D.
Jim Cummins, Ph.D.
Pat Cunningham, Ph.D.
Elfrieda Hiebert, Ph.D.
Pamela Mason, Ed.D.
Ernest Morrell, Ph.D.
P. David Pearson, Ph.D.
Frank Serafini, Ph.D.
Alfred Tatum, Ph.D.
Sharon Vaughn, Ph.D.
Judy Wallis, Ed.D.
Lee Wright, Ed.D.

UNIT 5

CONTENTS

Outside My Door

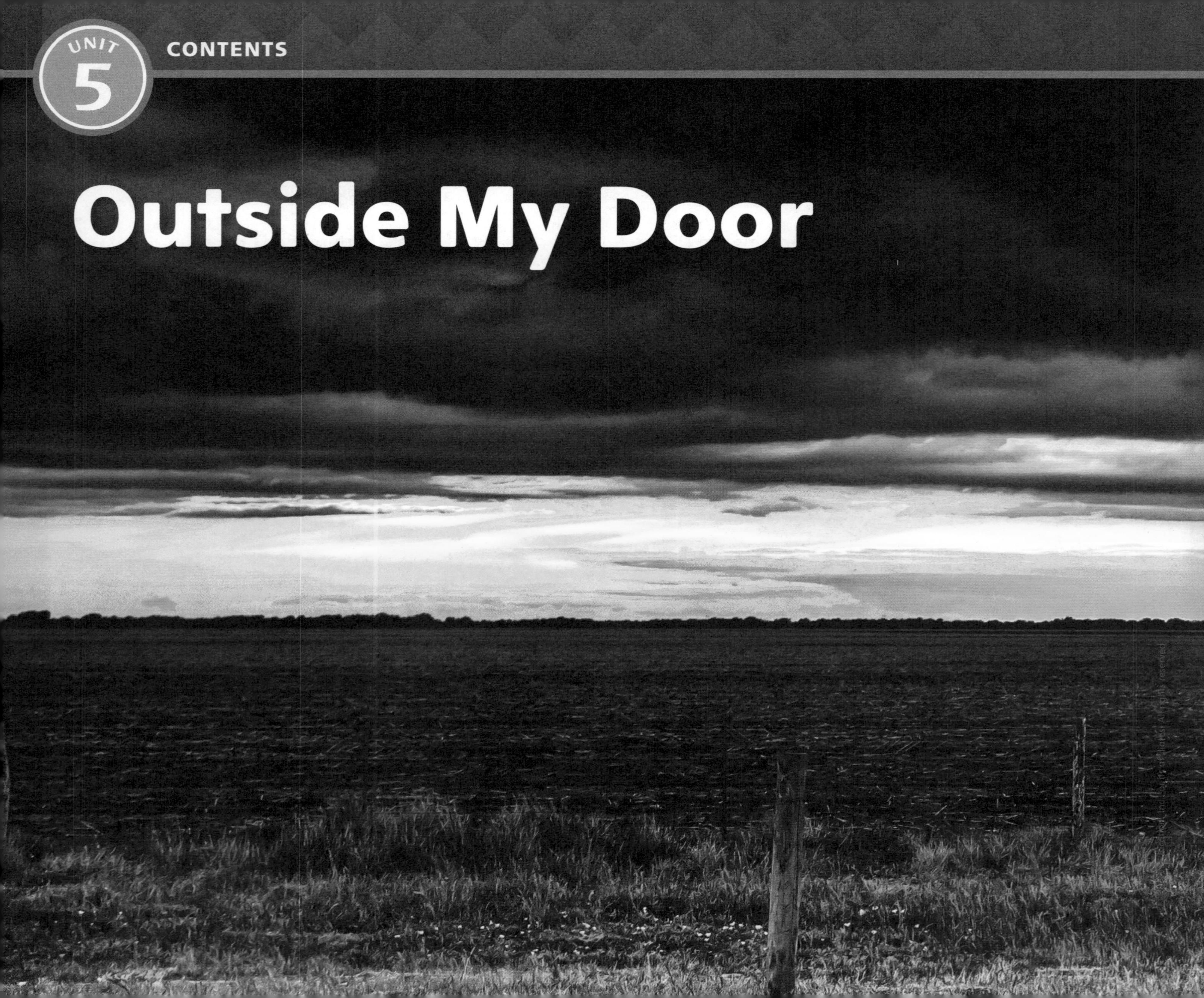

Outside My Door

Essential Question

What can we learn from the weather?

Watch

"Weather!" to learn about different kinds of weather.

TURN and TALK

What kinds of weather do we get?

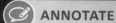

Go ONLINE for all lessons.

VIDEO

AUDIO

GAME

ANNOTATE

BOOK

RESEARCH

Reading Workshop

Reading-Writing Bridge

Writing Workshop

Project-Based Inquiry

Independent Reading

Try these strategies when you do not know a word.

1. Sound it out.
2. Look for word parts you know.
3. Look for clues in the text and pictures.

meaning

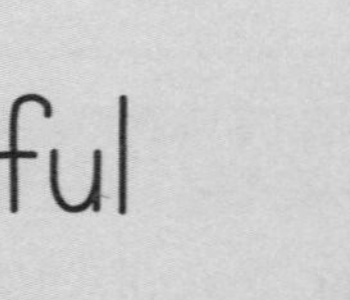

ful

Directions Read aloud the information with students and discuss the strategies for figuring out an unknown word in a text. Say: Use these strategies as you read on your own.

My Independent Reading Log

Date	Book	Pages Read	My Ratings

Directions Have students select a text and interact independently with it for increasing periods of time. Tell them to read a few more pages every day and to use strategies such as looking for clues in the text and pictures to figure out unknown words as they read. Then have students complete the chart.

Unit Goals

In this unit, you will

- ○ read informational texts
- △ write a literary nonfiction text
- □ talk about what we can learn from the weather

Circle the pictures of weather.

Directions Read and discuss the unit goals with students. Then discuss different kinds of weather and have students circle the pictures that show a kind of weather.

Academic Vocabulary

MY TURN Match

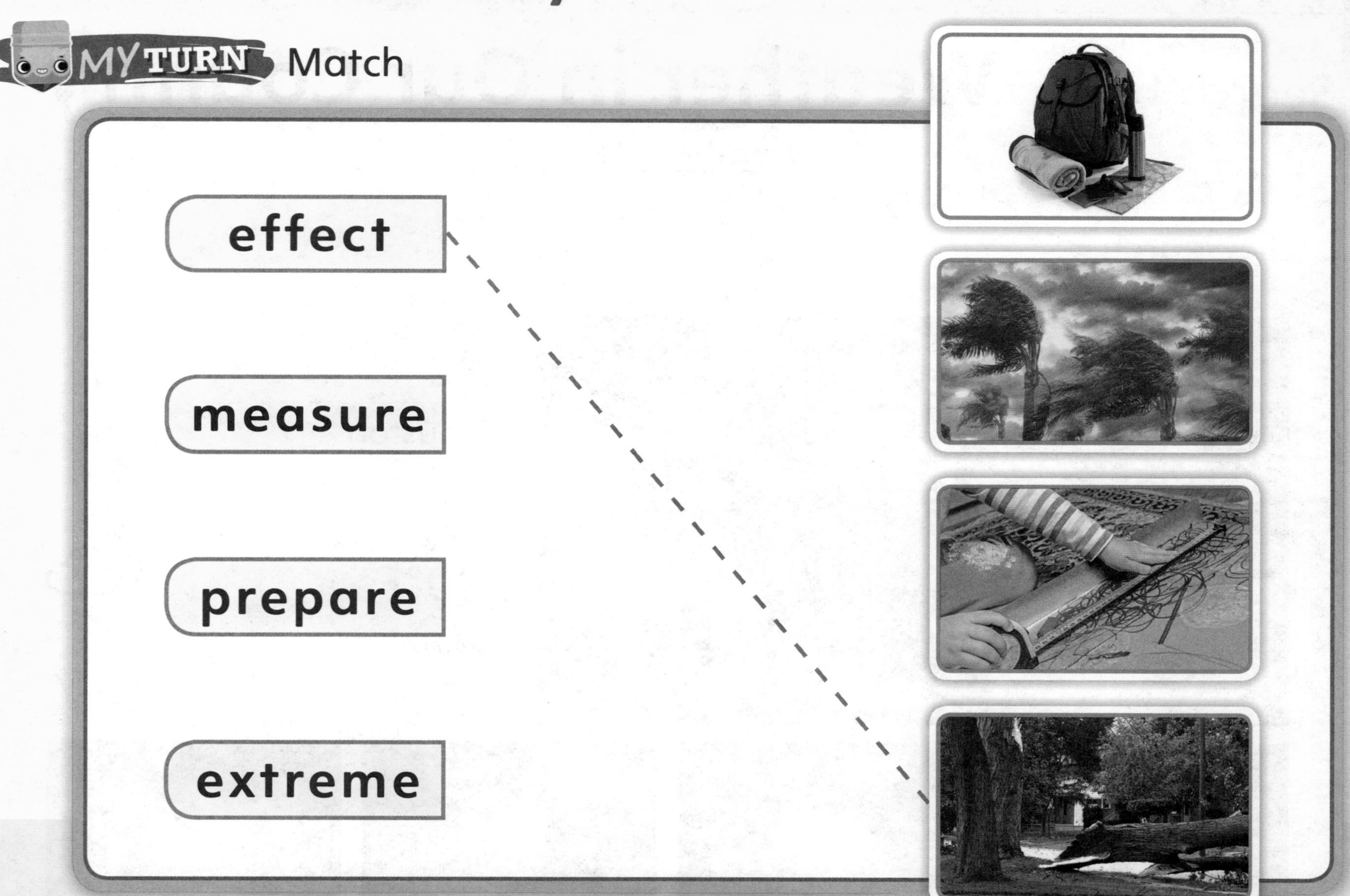

Directions Read the Academic Vocabulary words to students and discuss the meanings of the words. Then discuss what the pictures show. Have students match each word to the picture that shows a meaning of the word.

Read Together

Address bar

http://www.url.here

Weather in Our Country

Search box

Weather Alerts

Link

Search

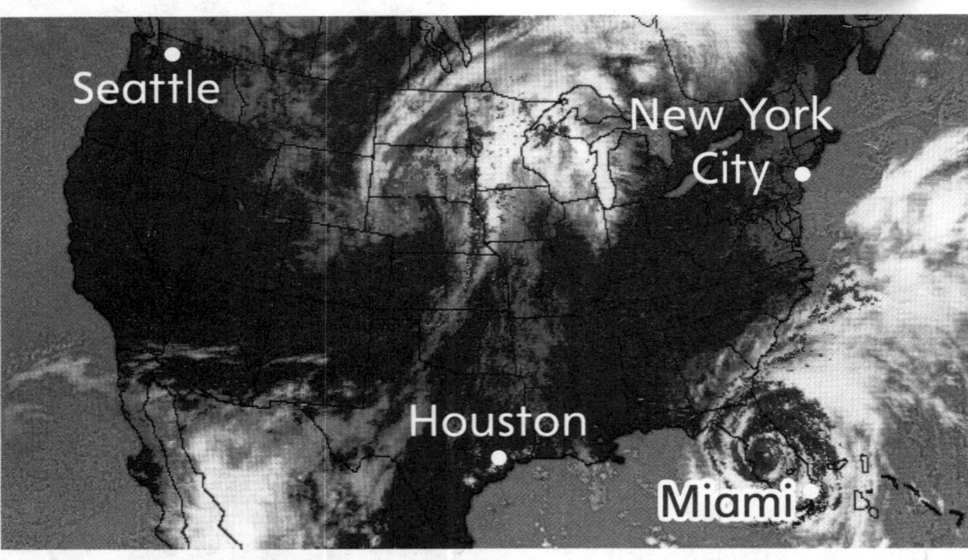

Seattle
42°F

Houston
69°F

New York City
30°F

Miami
78°F

Video

Weekly Question

How have people learned to live in bad weather?

http://www.url.here

What kinds of weather are happening across the country? You can use a Web site to find out!

Search

Local Weather

Today	Saturday	Sunday

TURN and TALK Talk about what you can learn from the different parts of the Web site.

Directions Have students look at the Web site as you read aloud the text and labels. Say: Web sites have certain characteristics, such as an address bar at the top and a search box. Ask students to find the characteristics of a Web site in the text. Then have partners talk about what they can learn from the different parts of the Web site.

Words for Cc, Tt

Read and sort

top	cub	cape	time

can

cape

tin

Directions Have students read the word at the top of each column and identify the beginning letter and sound. Then ask students to read the words in the word bank and sort them by writing each word in the column for the word that begins with the same letter and sound.

Words for Short and Long o

Read and circle

She had a ___.  rob  robe

It can ___.  hop hope

I ___ my bike.  rod rode

Directions Remind students that the vowel pattern *o_e* can make the long *o* vowel sound and the letter *o* can make the short *o* sound. Have students read each sentence and the answer choices. Ask them to circle the word that completes each sentence.

Words for Short and Long o, Cc, Tt

Read

I can walk home.

I will spin the top.

I open the tan box.

I cut a hole.

Directions Remind students that the vowel pattern *o_e* can make the long *o* sound and the letter *o* can make the short *o* sound. Also review that the letter *c* can stand for /k/ and *t* stands for /t/. Have partners take turns reading the sentences.

My Words to Know

be	saw	our

My Sentences to Read

I saw a cat.

Can she be mine?

Come and see our home!

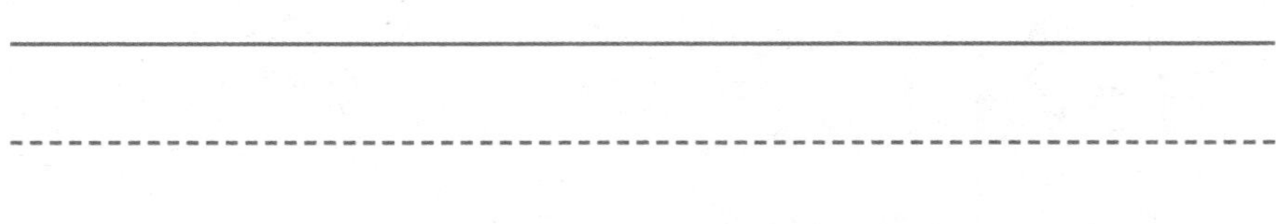

Directions Have students read the high-frequency words in the word bank. Then have them read the sentences and underline the high-frequency words. Say: Now you will write one of the words on the lines. Tell students to form the letters correctly using appropriate directionality.

Tif and Cole

AUDIO

Audio with Highlighting

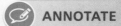

ANNOTATE

Look at it come down!

Tif did not want to be wet.

"What can we do?" said Cole.

Underline the words with the short **o** sound.

Tif had on a blue one.

Cole had on a green one.

"Let us go to our spot!" said Tif.

Tif saw a man with a vest.

Cole saw some black smoke.

They went to a slope.

Highlight the words with the long **o** sound.

Tif and Cole made a round home.

They got on a sled.

They had a lot of fun!

Sentences I Can Read

Read and draw

1. Draw a bed for a cat.
2. Draw a bone for a pup.
3. Draw a top for a kid.

1 2 3

Directions Have students read the sentences. Then have them follow the directions to draw pictures in the boxes.

Sentences I Can Read

Read and write

Tom	box	drove

Tom drove the van.

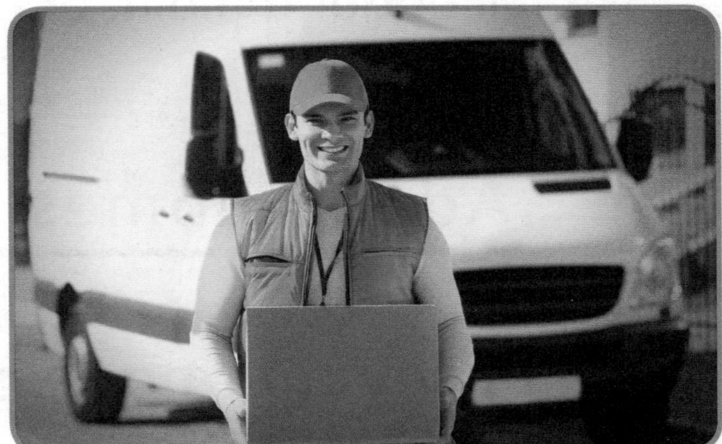

He got a ______.

Now ______ can go home.

Directions Ask students to read the words and sentences. Then have them write the words to complete the sentences. Finally, have students read the completed sentences.

My Learning Goal

I can read informational text.

SPOTLIGHT ON GENRE

Informational Text

Informational text uses details in words and pictures to tell about a main, or central, idea.

Main Idea — Adobe homes are special.

Detail — They are made of mud.

TURN and TALK Talk about details you learned about adobe homes.

Directions Read the genre information and model text to students. Have them find the characteristics of informational text, such as the main idea and supporting details in the text and graphic. Then have partners discuss what they learned about adobe homes from the model text.

Informational Text Anchor Chart

Details

mud

Words

Weather Around the World

Preview Vocabulary

snow	rainy	windy	weather

Read

Listen to the title and look at the pictures. What do you predict the text will be about?

Meet the Author

André Ngāpō is a writer, musician, and teacher from New Zealand. He writes about people, places, feelings, and moods. He also shares stories about the native Māori people.

Read Together

Genre Informational Text

Weather Around the World

written by André Ngāpō

AUDIO

Audio with Highlighting

ANNOTATE

Many places in the world
have extreme weather.
Some places are very cold.
Some places are very hot.

CLOSE READ

What place does the first picture show? Underline the words that name the place.

Some places are very rainy.
Some places are very windy.
People find ways to live in
all of these places.

In Alaska, it is very cold.
People make huts out of snow.
The walls block out the cold winds.

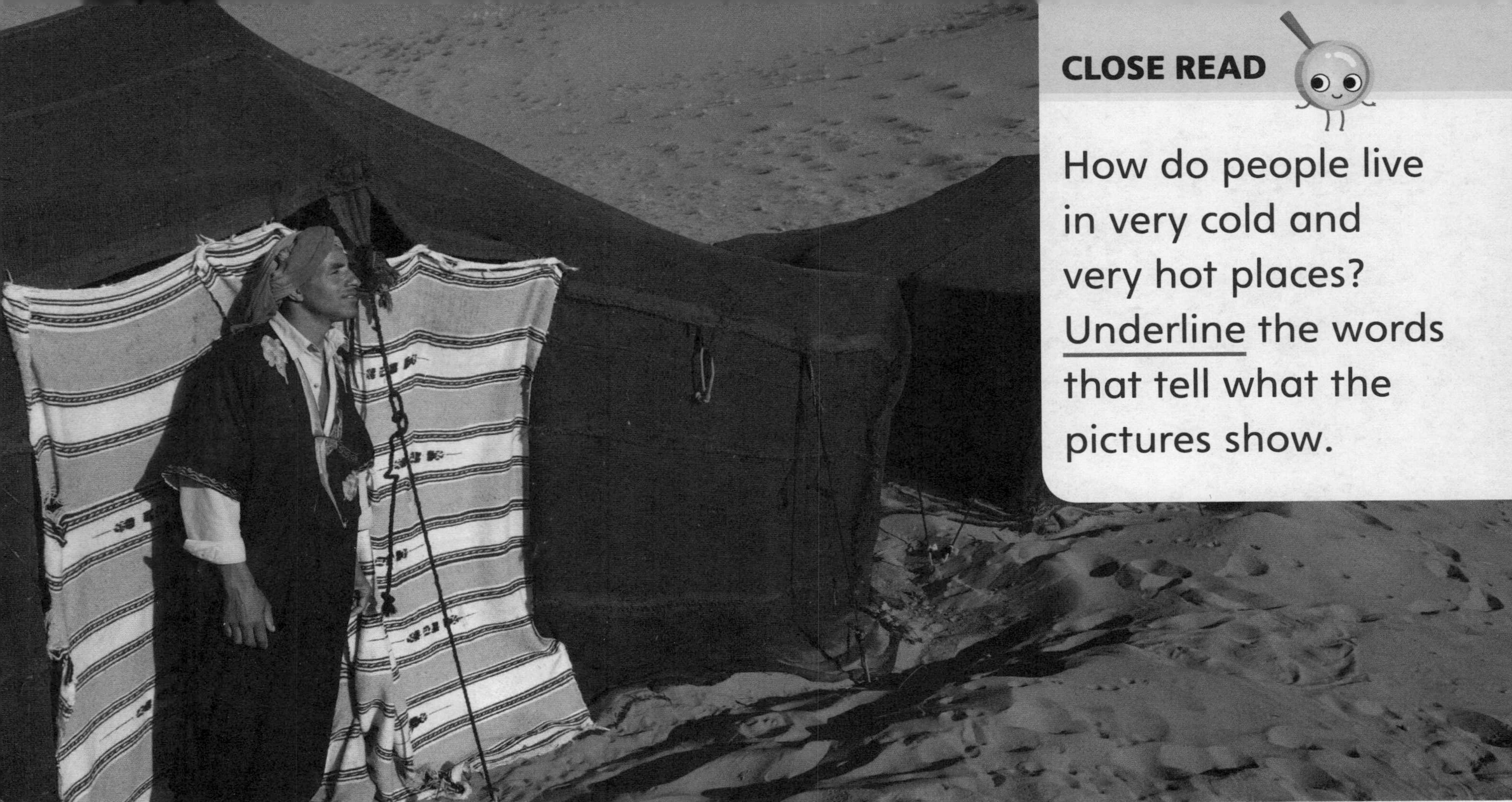

CLOSE READ

How do people live in very cold and very hot places? Underline the words that tell what the pictures show.

In the desert, it is often very hot.
People live in tents.
The tents keep the hot air out.

In China, it can be very rainy.
People make hats out of plants.
They wear the hats when they work.

CLOSE READ

Why do people in China wear hats when they work? Highlight the words that help you know the answer. Use the picture too.

In Antarctica, it is very windy. Scientists live and work in buildings of many shapes and sizes.

Around the world, people find ways to live with extreme weather.

Choose a place you just read about.
What would you do to be able to live there?

Develop Vocabulary

Draw and write

rainy	windy

Directions Read the vocabulary words aloud to students. Have them draw a picture to show the meaning of each word. Then have them write a sentence with one of the words.

Check for Understanding

Write

1. What is the main idea of the text?

2. Why does the author ask a question at the end?

3. How are homes in Alaska and the desert alike?

Directions Read aloud the questions and have students write their responses. Then ask students to discuss their answer to question 1 and use it to confirm the prediction they made before reading.

Connect Text and Illustrations

The pictures in a text can show more details about what the words say.

Write

Directions Have students look at each picture and write the idea from the text that the picture shows. Remind them to go back to what they underlined in the text. Then have students discuss additional details the pictures show that are not in the text.

Make Inferences

Draw and write

Directions Remind students that they can use details in the text and what they already know to make inferences. Ask: Why do people in China wear hats to help them work? Have students draw the answer to the question and write evidence from the text that supports their response. Remind students to use what they highlighted.

Reflect and Share

Draw

Weekly Question

How have people learned to live in bad weather?

Directions Tell students they read about weather in different parts of the world. Have students think about other texts they have read about weather. Say: You can respond to texts by drawing a picture that shows what you have learned. Have students respond to sources by drawing a type of weather from this text and a type of weather from another text they have read.

I can use words to tell about informational text.

My Learning Goal

Academic Vocabulary

effect	measure	prepare	extreme

Write

I am ______________________

for school.

prepared	unprepared

Directions Read the sentence and answer choices to students. Discuss the meanings of the word *prepare* and the related words *prepared* and *unprepared*. Then have students write the word that best completes the sentence on the lines.

Spell Words

Sort and spell

be	cat	tap
not	saw	hat

cat

Directions Say: Short *a* is often spelled *a* and short *o* is often spelled *o* in words with three letters. Some words do not follow a pattern, so you have to remember how to spell them. **Have students determine if each word follows the CVC pattern. Then have them spell and write the CVC words in the left column and the high-frequency words in the right column.**

Read Like a Writer, Write for a Reader

Write

1. Look at the picture of Antarctica. How does it help you understand the weather there?

2. What picture could you use to show the weather where you live?

Directions Read the first item and have students look at the photo before writing their response. Have them discuss how the author uses photos in the text to achieve his purpose. Then read the second item and ask students to think about what the weather is like where they live. Have them write their response on the lines.

Capitalization

A sentence always begins with a **capital letter**.

The word **I** is always a capital letter.

What should **I** wear today?

Tell why each letter is capitalized.

Underline and write

how can i stay dry?

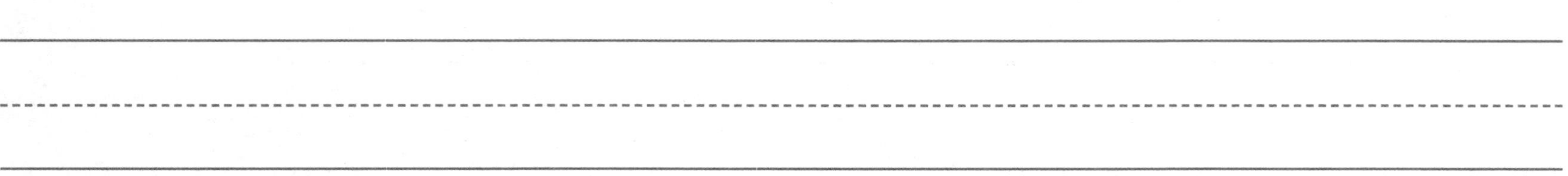

Directions Read aloud the information and ask partners to talk about why each bold letter in the example sentence is capitalized. Then have students edit the practice sentence by underlining the letters that should be capitalized. Ask them to rewrite the sentence on the lines, capitalizing the underlined letters.

I can write a nonfiction text.

My Learning Goal

Question and Answer Book

Some books ask **questions** about a topic.

Then they **answer** the questions.

The answers tell information.

Thunderstorms

Question — What is a thunderstorm?

Answer — It is a storm with thunder and lightning.

Directions Read aloud the student model and discuss the characteristics of a question and answer book.

Think of Ideas

Question and answer books tell about a **topic.**

Authors write about topics they know.

Draw

Directions Have students participate in a class discussion to think of ideas for writing. Then have students draw topics they know about.

Plan Your Question and Answer Book

Draw or write

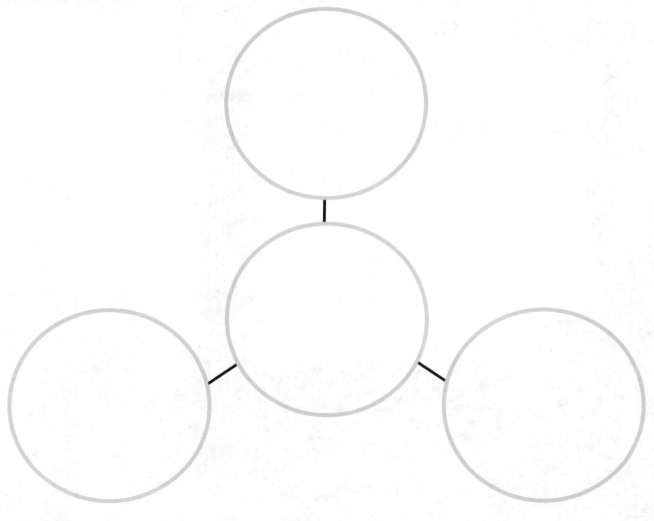

Directions Tell students that graphic organizers can help them plan what they will write. Have students write a word or draw a picture in the center circle to name a topic. Then ask them to write or draw details they can tell about the topic in the outer circles.

Living in the Desert

A desert is very hot and dry.
How do cactuses grow there?

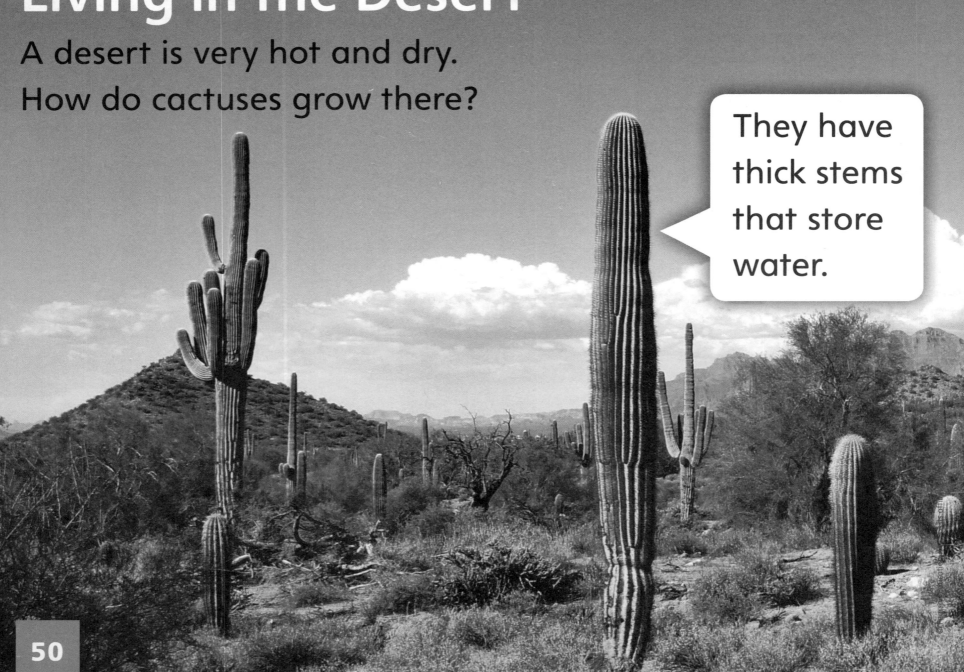

They have thick stems that store water.

Weekly Question

What helps plants live in hot climates?

Their roots take in water quickly when it rains.

Write

It has ________________________________.

Directions Read the text and have students look at the pictures. Then have them interact with the source by using the information they learned to write an answer to the following question: What helps a cactus live in the desert?

Words for Bb, Jj

Read and write

The _at is brown. bat

This is a fast _et.

It can _uzz by the _ug.

Directions Ask students to name the pictures and read the sentences. Then have them write the word for each picture on the lines to complete each sentence.

Initial and Final Blends

Read and write

Tap the drum.

Look at the ______.

I have a ______.

Directions Have students read each sentence and write the word for the picture on the lines. Then have them read the completed sentences.

Words for Bb, Jj, Initial and Final Blends

Read

Clap one time.

Step one time.

Jump up.

Bend down.

Directions Remind students that *b* makes the sound /b/, *j* makes the sound /j/, and consonant blends are two or more consonants with sounds that blend together in a word. Have partners take turns reading the sentences and performing the actions.

My Words to Know

eat	soon	walk

My Sentences to Read

Jen and Mom go on a walk.

They will go home soon.

It is time to eat.

Directions Say: We have to remember and practice some words, such as *eat*, *soon*, and *walk*. Have students read the high-frequency words. Then have them read the sentences and underline the high-frequency words in the sentences.

They Get Big!

AUDIO

Audio with Highlighting

ANNOTATE

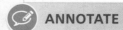

Bud had a little plant.

It sat in the hot sun.

Underline the words with the **b** sound.

Bud gave the plant a drip.

He let it sit.

Soon the plant got big!

Mom got Jen a little cat.

Jen gave the cat a bite to eat.

Soon the cat got big!

Highlight the words with the **j** sound.

Jake and Dad went for a walk.

They saw a little bug in a pond.

"Will the bug get big?" asked Jake.

Sentences I Can Read

Read and write

sl	mp	pr

Hope got a big pr______ize.

Bob will ______ide down.

June can ju______ rope.

Directions Have students read the sentences and describe what is happening in the pictures. Then have them write the consonant blend from the word bank that best completes each word. Finally, have students read the completed sentences.

Sentences I Can Read

Read and write

☒ Sal got a pretty bike.

☐ Sal got a pretty bat.

☐ The jug will go up.

☐ The jet will go up.

☐ The crab is in the sand.

☐ The crab is in the hand.

Directions Ask students to look at the first picture. Then have them read the first pair of sentences. Ask students to write an X in the box by the sentence that tells about the picture. Continue with the other pictures and sentences.

My Learning Goal

I can read informational text.

SPOTLIGHT ON GENRE

Informational Text

Informational texts can be organized in different ways.
They can tell the **steps in a sequence**.

First	Next	Last
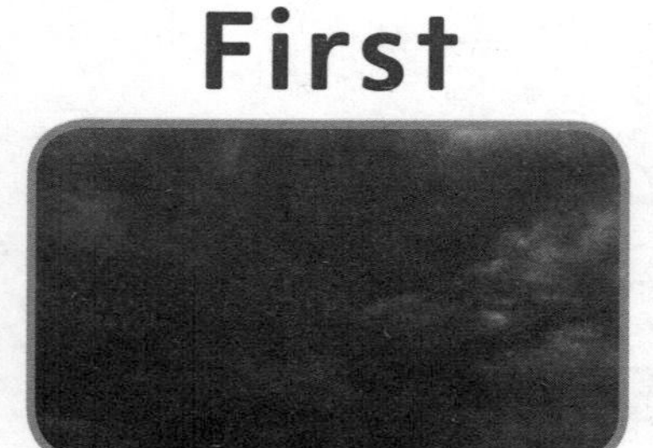		

Talk about the steps in order.

Directions Read the genre information aloud to students and explain that when an informational text tells steps in a sequence, it tells what happens first, next, and last. Have students look at the pictures and talk about what happens first, next, and last during a rainstorm.

Informational Text Anchor Chart

First

Next

Last

A Desert in Bloom

Preview Vocabulary

soil	bloom	ground	desert

Read

Read the text and look at the pictures to find out how flowers grow in the desert.

Meet the Author

Justin Scott Parr writes stories about science, nature, and imagination. His characters joke with dinosaurs, play with insects, and chase stars across the solar system.

Read Together

Genre Informational Text

A Desert in Bloom

written by Justin Scott Parr

AUDIO

Audio with Highlighting

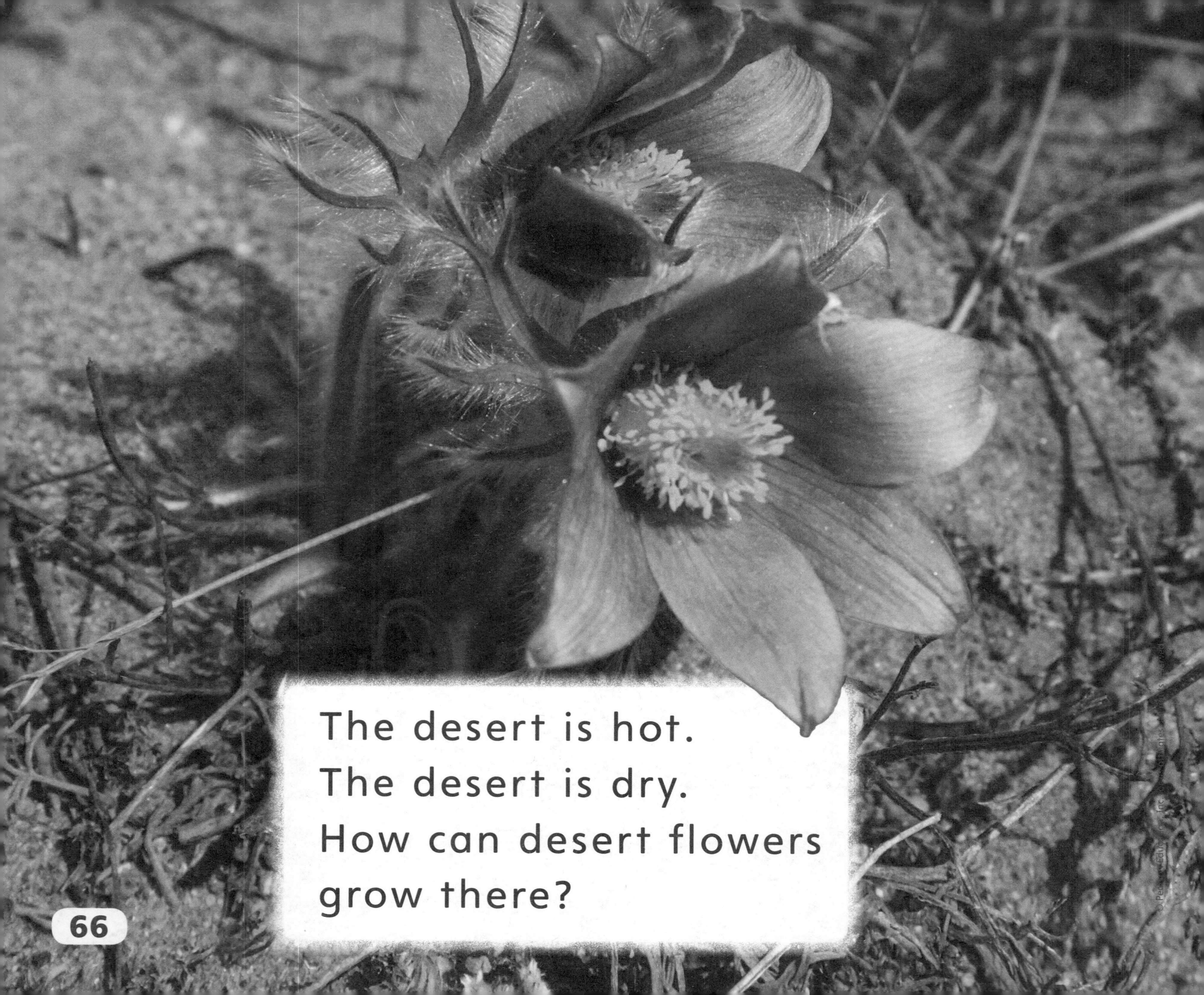

The desert is hot.
The desert is dry.
How can desert flowers
grow there?

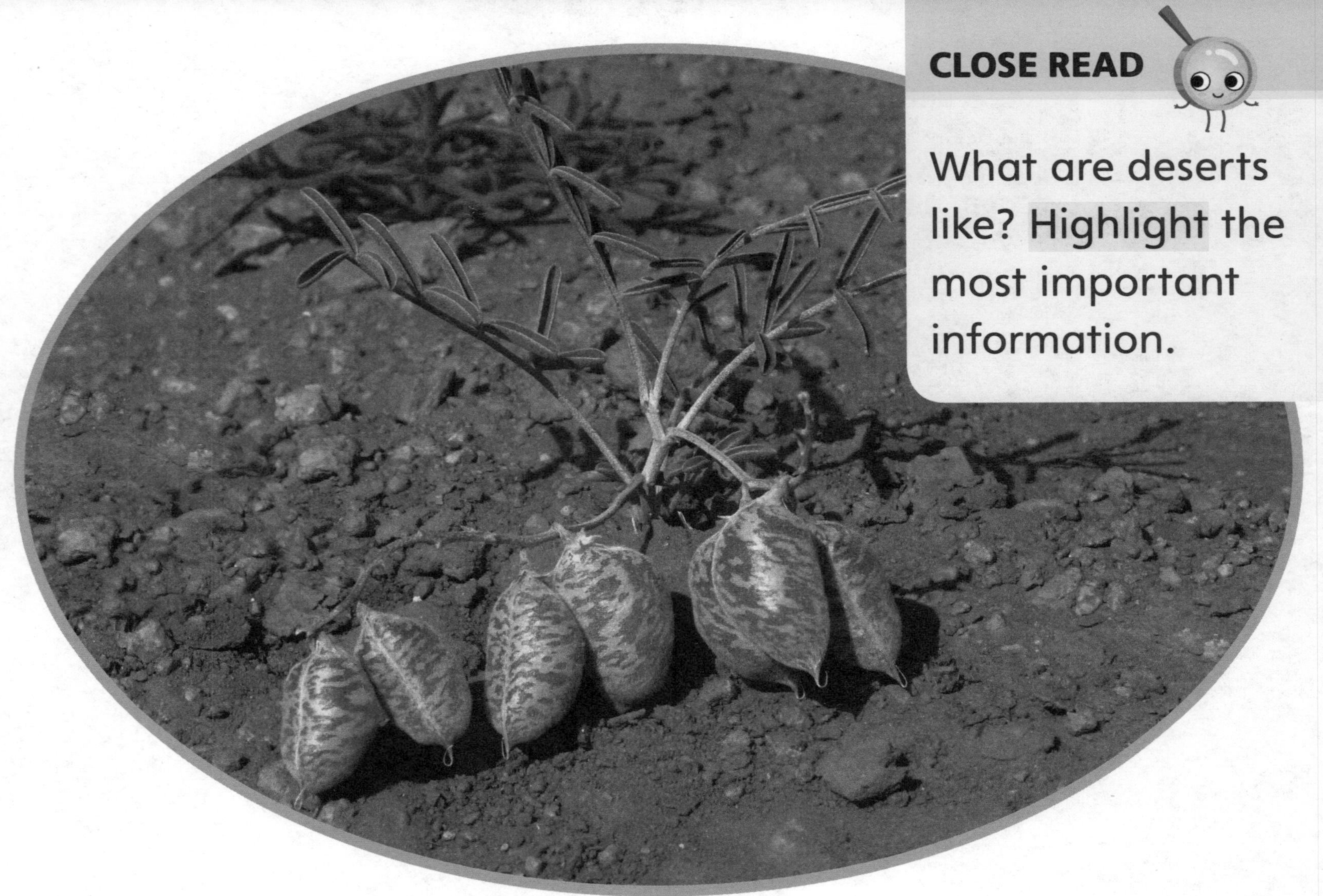

CLOSE READ

What are deserts like? Highlight the most important information.

The desert soil is full of seeds.

In summer, the ground is
hot and dry.
The seeds do not grow.

CLOSE READ

What do these pages tell about how flowers grow? Underline the words that tell when the steps happen.

In fall, the ground gets cool
from cloudy days.
The seeds do not grow.

In winter, the ground gets soaked with rain.
The seeds start to grow.

CLOSE READ

What do these pages tell about how flowers grow? Underline the words that tell when the steps happen.

In spring, the ground gets warm from the sun.
Colorful flowers bloom.

When summer returns, it gets hot.
The flowers die.
Their seeds rest in the ground
until spring comes again.

CLOSE READ

What is the last thing that happens to flowers in the desert? Underline the words that tell when the last step happens.

Now you know how desert flowers grow!

Develop Vocabulary

soil | desert

bloom | soil

ground | desert

ground | bloom

Directions Read the words below each picture aloud. Have students circle the word that names the picture.

Check for Understanding

1. This text tells | a story | facts |.

2. Why do you think the author asks a question?

3. How do seeds start to grow in the desert?

Directions Read item 1 and the answer choices aloud to students. Have them circle the answer. Then read items 2 and 3 aloud and have students write their responses. Remind them to use text evidence.

Find Text Structure

Authors organize texts in different ways.

Some authors tell the steps in a sequence.

Write

Directions Say: Text structure is how the author organizes a text. When an author tells the steps in a sequence, the author often uses time words to tell when the steps happen. Have students look at the pictures and write when each step happens. Remind them to use what they underlined. Then discuss how the text structure contributes to the author's purpose in the text.

Find Important Details

Details tell more about a topic.

Draw and write

Directions Read the information aloud and say: Finding the most important details will help you better understand a topic. What important details do the words and pictures give about deserts? **Have students evaluate details in the text and draw and write the most important ones. Remind them to go back to what they highlighted.**

Reflect and Share

TURN and TALK What is the desert like? What is another place you have read about like? Tell your opinion about the places.

An opinion is how you think or feel about a topic.

Weekly Question

What helps plants live in hot climates?

Directions Tell students they read about the desert. Ask them to think of other places they have read about. Have them respond to sources by talking about the places and telling which place they would most like to live in and why.

I can use words to tell about informational text.

My Learning Goal

Academic Vocabulary

effect	measure	prepare	extreme

Circle and underline

Desert weather is **extreme.**

severe gentle

Directions Read the sentence to students and discuss the meaning of the word *extreme*. Then read the word choices. Ask students to underline the word that has a similar meaning to *extreme* and circle the word that has the opposite meaning.

Spell Words

Sort and spell

flag	eat	slip
trap	stop	walk

flag

Directions Say: Some words begin with a consonant blend. A consonant blend is two or more consonants that come together in a word, but each sound is heard. Have students determine if each word in the word bank follows the CCVC pattern. Then have them spell and write the CCVC words in the left column and the high-frequency words in the right column.

Read Like a Writer, Write for a Reader

Write

1. What words in the text help you picture what fall is like in the desert?

2. What other word could you use to help readers picture what the desert is like in the fall?

Directions Read the first question and have students look back at the text to find words to write on the lines. Then read the second question and have students write their response. Encourage them to look at the picture in the text for ideas.

End Punctuation

Every sentence ends with a **punctuation mark.**

Flowers grow in the desert.

Does it rain in the desert?

The flowers are pretty!

MY TURN Write

It is much too hot ______

Flowers bloom in the spring ______

Is it raining ______

Directions Read aloud the information and example sentences. Tell students that declarative sentences end with a period, asking sentences end with a question mark, and exclamations end with an exclamation point. Then read the sentences and have students edit each one by writing the correct punctuation mark at the end.

I can write a nonfiction text.

My Learning Goal

What You Know About Your Topic

A question and answer book tells details about a topic.

Authors think about details they know before they write.

Write

What I Know

- There is thunder.
- There is lightning.
-

Directions Read aloud the sentences and have students think about what they know about thunderstorms. Have them organize ideas by dictating or writing a detail on the lines.

Compose Questions

A question begins with a **question word.**

A question ends with a **question mark.**

Write

Directions Review question words such as *who*, *what*, *where*, *when*, *why*, and *how*. Then have students look at the picture and write a question about thunderstorms. Tell them to include questions as they dictate or compose their question and answer books.

Compose Answers

Think about what you know to answer your questions.

You can also find answers to your questions in books.

End each sentence with a period.

Write

How can we protect ourselves during a thunderstorm?

Directions Read the question and have students use what they know to write an answer. Remind them to end their sentence with a period. Tell students to include answers as they dictate or compose their question and answer books.

Weather Poems

Snowflakes

The snowflakes are falling
by ones and by twos.
There's snow on my jacket
and snow on my shoes.
There's snow on the bushes
and snow on the trees.
It's snowing on everything
now, if you please.

written by
Leroy F. Jackson

Weekly Question

WEEK 3

How do we describe weather?

Rain on the Green Grass

Rain on the green grass,
and rain on the tree,
rain on the housetop,
but not on me!

Circle a word in each poem that tells about the weather.

Directions Read the poems to students. Have them interact with the poems by circling words that describe, or tell about, the weather.

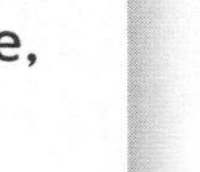

Words for Gg, Qq

Read and write

game	gate	quiz

We had a quiz.

Can you open the ______________?

We like this ______________.

Directions Have students tell what they see in each picture. Then have them read each sentence. Ask them to complete each sentence by writing the best word from the word bank on the lines.

Words for Short and Long a

Read

at	hat	ham	am
ape	cape	cave	save
an	tan	ran	rag
plate	late	lake	make

Directions Remind students that the letter *a* can make the short *a* sound and the vowel pattern *a_e* can make the long *a* sound. Say: We can make new words by changing, adding, or deleting letters. Have partners take turns reading the words and naming the letters that were changed, added, or deleted to make new words.

Words for Short and Long a, Gg, Qq

Jane will do a craft.

She can make a quilt.

It is a gift for Dave.

He will clap!

Directions Remind students that the letter *a* can make the short *a* sound, the vowel pattern *a_e* can make the long *a* sound, the letter *g* can make the /g/ sound, and the letters *qu* make the /kw/ sound. Have students read the sentences. Ask them to underline the words with short or long *a* and circle the words with *g* or *q*.

My Words to Know

who	into	there

My Sentences to Read

Let us go into my home.

We can play there.

Who will come?

Directions Have students read the high-frequency words. Then have them read the sentences and underline the high-frequency words in the sentences. Finally, have students write one of the words on the lines. Tell them to form the letters correctly using appropriate directionality.

Who Am I?

There is a game we like!

I am little and white.

I can be made into a man.

Who am I?

AUDIO

Audio with Highlighting

ANNOTATE

Underline the words with the long **a** sound.

Gil, you are a flake!

Now I will go.

I am big and yellow.

I get quite hot.

Who am I?

Highlight the words with the letter **g**.

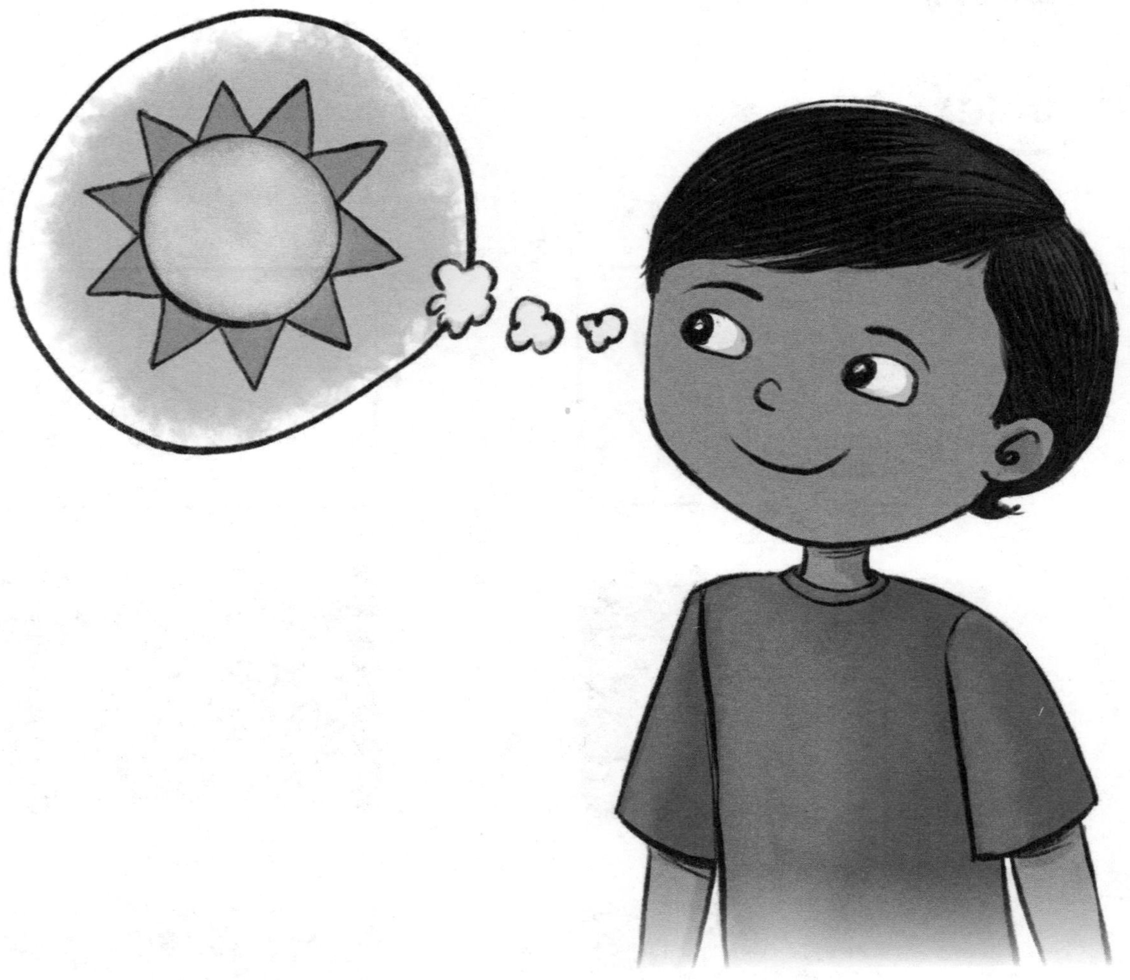

Quade, you are the sun.

This is a fun game!

Sentences I Can Read

Read and circle

The quilt is pretty.

Play the game.

They go in the lake.

Directions Say: Read the first sentence. Now look at the pictures. Circle the picture that matches the sentence. Have students continue with the remaining sentences.

Sentences I Can Read

Read and write

quit!	We	not	will

She will rake a pile.

I can fill the bag.

He will dig up a stone.

Directions Ask students to read the sentences. Have them use the words in the word bank to write the last sentence for the story. Alternatively, students may wish to write their own last sentence.

My Learning Goal I can read about weather.

Poetry

A **poem** uses words to describe something.
Many poems have **rhyming words** and **rhythm,** or a beat.

Rhyming Words

The itsy, bitsy spider
went up the water spout.
Down came the rain
and washed the spider out.

TURN and TALK Talk about how this poem is different from an informational text about weather.

Directions Read aloud the genre information and model text and remind students that rhyming words have the same middle and ending sounds. Have them discuss the rhythm and rhyming words in the nursery rhyme. Then have partners talk about how the poem is different from an informational text.

Poetry Anchor Chart

Rhythm

Rhyming Words

Poetry Collection

Preview Vocabulary

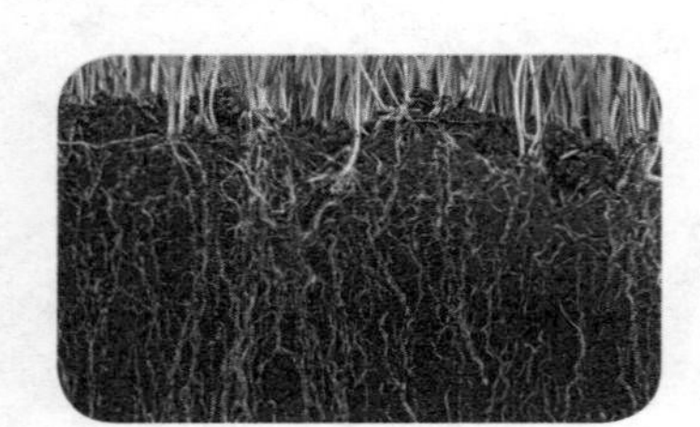		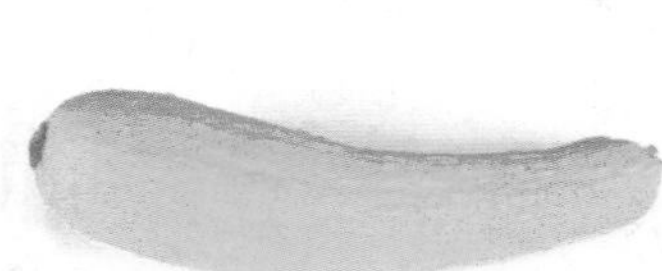	
roots	mound	squash	shoots

Read

Read the poems to discover new ways to describe weather.

Meet the Author

Eric Gansworth (Eel Clan) is a member of the Onondaga Nation. He grew up near Niagara Falls in New York. He writes fiction and poetry for young people and adults.

Poetry Collection

"Wehh-dooj"
(It's Raining)

"Ees-aw-hah' Ees-aeh"
(The Sun Shining)

written by Eric Gansworth

illustrated by Talitha Shipman

AUDIO

Audio with Highlighting

ANNOTATE

"Wehh-dooj" (It's Raining)

We feel "Wehh-dooj"
Water fills the air
And soaks into our hair

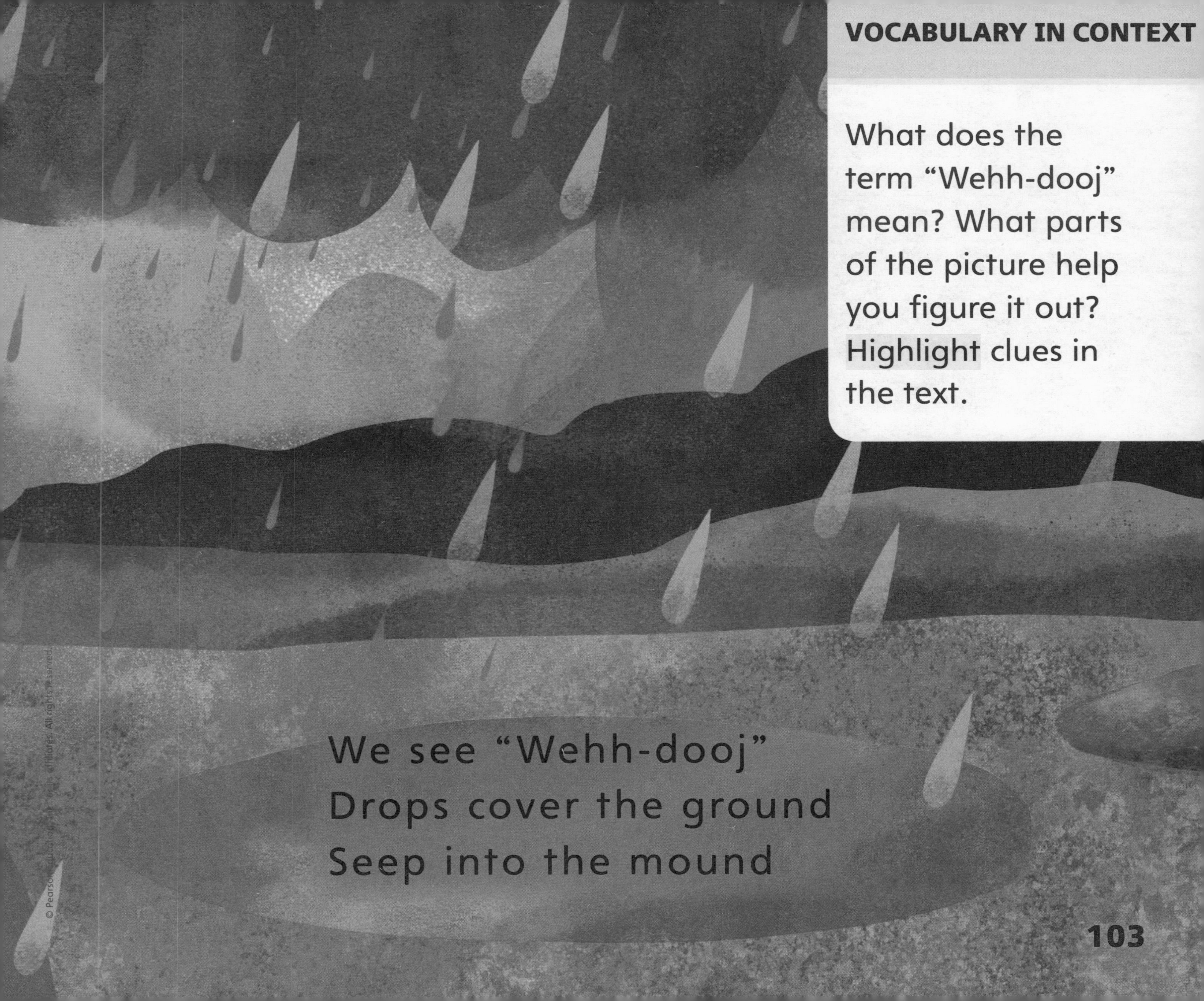

VOCABULARY IN CONTEXT

What does the term "Wehh-dooj" mean? What parts of the picture help you figure it out? Highlight clues in the text.

We see "Wehh-dooj"
Drops cover the ground
Seep into the mound

We feel "Wehh-dooj"
Where we plant three seeds
Together like beads

CLOSE READ

Which words help you picture the seeds? Highlight the words.

They love "Wehh-dooj"
Corn, beans, and squash
Need the rain to wash

"Ees-aw-hah' Ees-aeh" (The Sun Shining)

We feel "Ees-aw-hah' Ees-aeh"
On our shirt
And in the mound of dirt

CLOSE READ

Which words rhyme, or have the same ending sounds? Underline the rhyming words. Clap the rhythm.

We see "Ees-aw-hah' Ees-aeh"
And color the sky
As birds fly by

We watch “Ees-aw-hah’ Ees-aeh”
On fresh new shoots
Growing up from their roots

CLOSE READ

Which words help you picture the shoots? Highlight the words.

They love "Ees-aw-hah' Ees-aeh"
Three sisters together
Give us food forever

Develop Vocabulary

Match

mound

roots

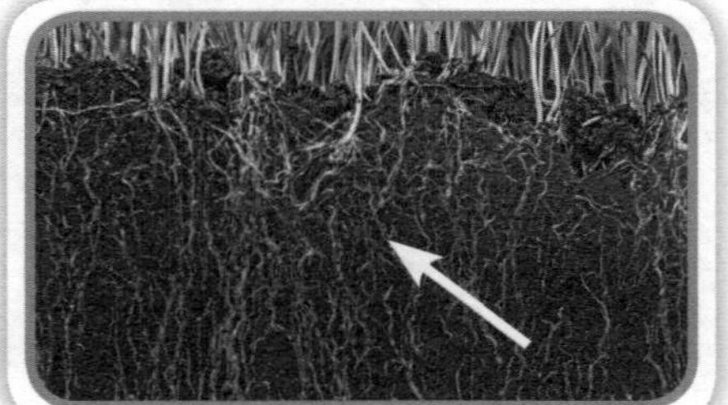

squash

shoots

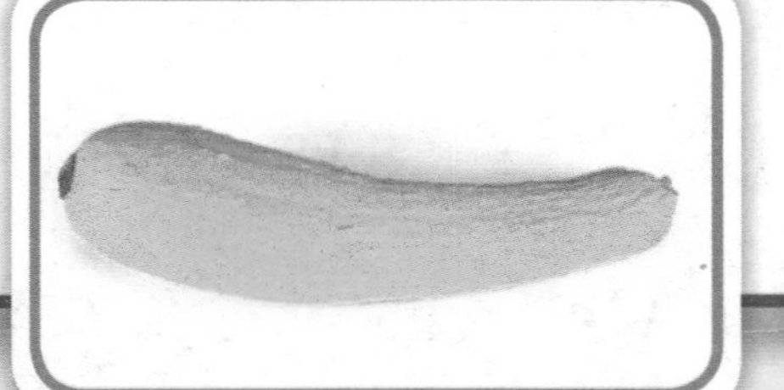

Directions Read the vocabulary words aloud to students. Then have them draw a line from each word to the matching picture.

Check for Understanding

Write

1. How do you know these are poems?

2. How does the author help you picture rain?

3. Why do the children love "Ees-aw-hah' Ees-aeh"?

Directions Read each question aloud and have students write their responses. Then discuss responses.

Discuss Rhyme and Rhythm

Poems often have **rhyming words**.

Poems can also have **rhythm**, or a beat.

dirt

by

Clap

Directions Tell students that rhyming words have the same middle and ending sounds and that rhythm is a strong beat. Discuss rhyme and rhythm in the poems with students. Then read each word aloud and have them circle the picture word that rhymes. Remind students to use what they underlined in the text. Finally, read aloud a stanza from one of the poems as students clap the rhythm.

Visualize Details

Draw

seeds	shoots

Directions Remind students they can use details in a text to visualize, or picture in their mind, what is happening. Ask them to discuss words the author uses that help them picture the seeds and shoots in the poems. Then have students draw what they picture. Remind them to use what they highlighted in the text.

Reflect and Share

MY TURN Write

Weekly Question

How do we describe weather?

Directions Tell students they read about rainy and sunny weather. Ask them to think of other texts they have read about rainy and sunny weather. Have students respond to sources by writing about one type of weather using details from the poems and from another text.

I can use words to make connections.

My Learning Goal

Academic Vocabulary

effect	measure	prepare	extreme

Circle

One **effect** rain can have is helping plants to grow.

get ready

something that happens

Directions Read the sentence and the answer choices to students. Ask them to use clues in the sentence to determine the meaning of the word *effect*. Have students circle the meaning of the word.

Spell Words

Sort and spell

at	am	an
who	into	as

at

Directions Say: Short *a* is often spelled *a* in words with two letters. Some words do not follow a pattern, so you have to remember how to spell them. Have students determine if each word follows the VC pattern. Then have them spell and write the VC words in the left column and the high-frequency words in the right column.

Read Like a Writer, Write for a Reader

Write

1. What word does the author use that rhymes with **air?**

2. Pretend you are writing the poem. What other words could you use that rhyme with **air?**

Directions Discuss rhyming words in the poems with students. Then read the first question. Have students identify and write the word that rhymes with *air.* Read the second question and ask students to produce other rhyming words for *air*.

Complete Sentences

A **complete sentence** has a naming part and an action part.
It begins with a capital letter.
It ends with a punctuation mark.

The squash grows.

Circle and write

the sun

The shoots come up.

Directions Read the information and point out the naming part, action part, beginning capital letter, and ending punctuation mark in the example sentence. Then read the practice phrase and sentence. Have students circle the incomplete sentence and edit it by rewriting it as a complete sentence on the lines.

I can write a nonfiction text.

My Learning Goal

Organize Ideas

Authors **organize** their ideas, or put them in order.

Draw or write

Question	Answer

Directions Say: In a question and answer book, every question is followed by an answer. Tell students that authors can organize their ideas by talking and writing about their questions and answers. Have students talk with a partner about questions and answers they can write about their topic. Then have them draw or write a question and answer in the chart.

Compose an Introduction and Conclusion

An **introduction** is at the beginning of a text.

A **conclusion** is at the end.

Circle and underline

Let me tell you about thunderstorms.

What is a thunderstorm?

It is a storm with thunder and lightning.

There is a lot to learn about thunderstorms!

Directions Say: An introduction names the topic. A conclusion reminds readers about the topic. Ask students to circle the introduction and underline the conclusion in the sample text. Then have partners compare their answers and talk about how they identified the introduction and conclusion. Tell students to compose an introduction and conclusion in their question and answer books.

Graphics

A **graphic** shows more information about a topic.

Authors use graphics to add details.

Draw

Thunderstorms have thunder and lightning.

Directions Say: You can add details to the draft by drawing more about thunderstorms. Have students revise by adding details to the picture.

Read Together

Be Prepared!

It is good to be prepared for bad weather.

One way to prepare is by packing important supplies.

supply kit

clothing

flashlight

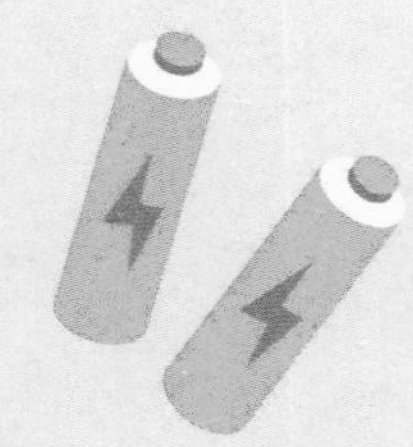

batteries

food

water

Weekly Question

How can we protect ourselves in bad weather?

radio

bandages

TURN and TALK Talk about the items in the supply kit. Then talk about other things you might pack to be prepared for bad weather.

Directions Read the text as students look at the pictures. Then have them interact with the source by discussing the pictured items and talking about other supplies they might pack. Encourage them to tell how each item might be helpful in bad weather.

Words for Kk, Ss

Read and write

sit	kit	bike

I have a bike.

He can ________.

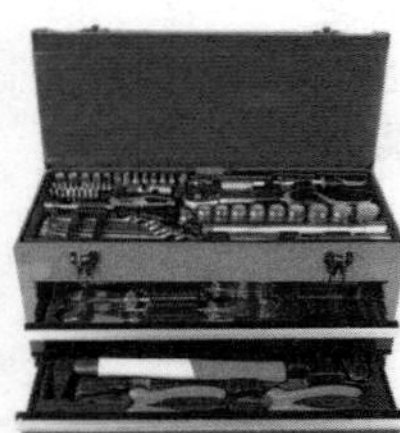

The ________ is big.

Directions Have students tell what they see in each picture. Then have them read each sentence. Ask them to complete each sentence by writing the best word from the word bank on the lines.

Words for Ww, Mm

Read and write

The grass is 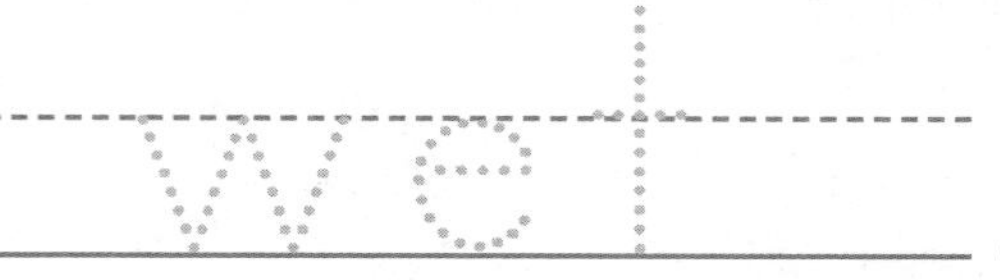 .

Look at the ______________.

I like the 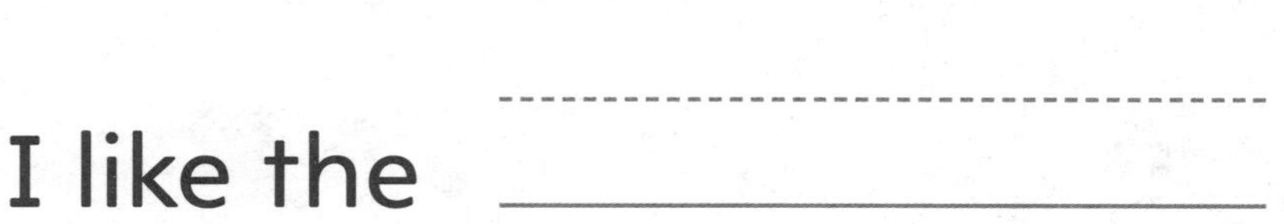 .

Directions Have students read each sentence and write the word for the picture to complete the sentence. Then have partners take turns reading the sentences.

Words for Kk, Ss, Ww, Mm

Read

	kid	kit	sit	it
	am	Sam	sad	mad
	web	wet	met	mat
	win	bin	bit	kit

Directions Tell students that we can make new words by changing, adding, or deleting letters. Have partners take turns reading the words in each row and naming the letters that were changed, added, or deleted to make new words.

My Words to Know

so	out	then

My Sentences to Read

We went out to play.

Then a drop came down.

So we went in.

Directions Say: We have to remember and practice some words, such as *so*, *out*, and *then*. Have students read the high-frequency words. Then have them read the sentences and underline the high-frequency words in the sentences.

Can We Be Out?

Kim was out with Dad.

They felt a drop so they went in.

Kim saw Wade get wet.

AUDIO

Audio with Highlighting

ANNOTATE

Underline the words with the letter **k**.

The sun was out.

Max went to the lake.

"I want to go for a swim," said Max.

Sid went for a walk.

The wind made her kite go.

Look at it go up!

Highlight the words with the **m** sound.

Look! It is white!

I make a man.

I will set my green hat on it.

Sentences I Can Read

MY TURN Read and write

mop	wet	kite	sand

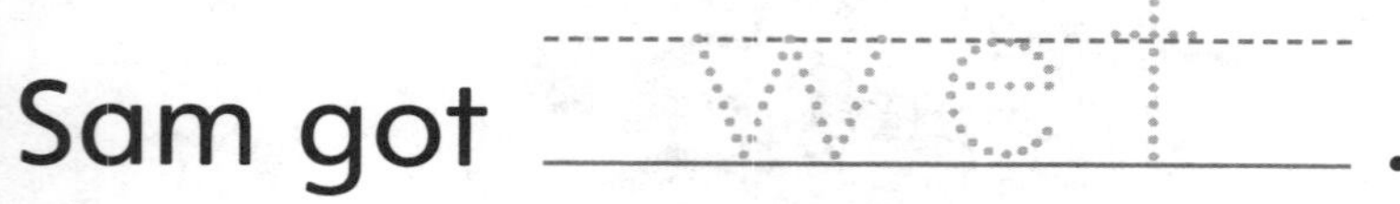

Sam got wet.

Dad will ________ it up.

They have a ________.

They play in the ________.

Directions Ask students to read the words and sentences. Then have them write the words to complete the sentences. Finally, have students read the completed sentences.

Sentences I Can Read

Read and write

k	s	w	m

The ___ un is out.

We ta ___ e a walk.

Mo ___ and I do not get ___ et.

Directions Review that printed words are made up of letters. Have students identify the letters in the bank. Then have them identify and read the words in the sentences. Explain that students will use the letters to complete the words in the sentences. Remind them to check that the sentences make sense when they complete the words.

My Learning Goal

I can read informational text.

SPOTLIGHT ON GENRE

Informational Text

Some informational texts tell the **steps in a sequence**. They can use numbers to show when steps happen.

TURN and TALK Talk about the steps. What should you do first, next, and last?

Directions Read the genre information aloud and review steps in a sequence. Then have students look at the pictures. Ask partners to talk about the steps they should follow to prepare to go outside in the rain.

Informational Text Anchor Chart

1

2

1

2

You can tell how steps are alike and different.

Tornado Action Plan

Preview Vocabulary

tornado	powerful

Read

Think about the title and the picture. What questions do you have before you read the text?

Meet the Author

Jill McDougall lives in South Australia. Her house is by the beach and every day she takes her dog for a paddle in the waves.

Directions Read aloud the title and have students look at the picture on the title page. Ask them to generate questions about the text before reading.

Genre Informational Text

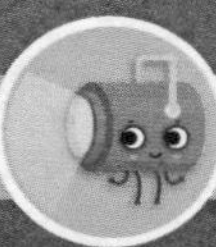

Tornado Action Plan

written by Jill McDougall

illustrated by André Ceolin

Audio with Highlighting

Tornadoes are powerful storms
with swirling winds.
They can cause a lot of damage.

CLOSE READ

What questions do you have about tornadoes? Highlight the words that help you answer your questions.

Take time to learn about tornadoes.
Make a plan to stay safe.
It is wise to be prepared.

Choose a safe area in your home. This could be a basement or even a closet.

CLOSE READ
What are two things you should do to prepare for a tornado? Underline what you should do.

Pack a bag.
Pack clothes and a flashlight.
Keep the bag in the safe area.

If a tornado comes:

1. Go straight to the safe area.
2. Wait for the tornado to pass.

A tornado action plan will keep you safe.

Blizzard Action Plan

Preview Vocabulary

strong	blizzard

Read and Compare

Read the text to find out how a blizzard action plan is similar to and different from a tornado action plan.

Meet the Illustrator

André Ceolin has illustrated more than 20 books for children and young adults. He started drawing when he was four years old and has been doing it ever since!

Genre Informational Text

written by Jill McDougall

illustrated by André Ceolin

Blizzard Action Plan

AUDIO

Audio with Highlighting

ANNOTATE

Blizzards are strong snowstorms.
They bring snow and wind.

CLOSE READ

What questions do you have about blizzards? Highlight the words that help you answer your questions.

Talk with your family about blizzards.
Make a plan to stay safe.
It is a good idea to be ready.

Pack a supply kit.
Pack water, food, and
a flashlight.

CLOSE READ

What should you do before a blizzard? What should you do during a blizzard? Underline the things you should do.

If a blizzard comes and you lose power:

1. Stay inside. Wear warm clothes.
2. Eat! Food helps keep you warm.

3. Play indoor games. Exercise helps keep you warm too.

VOCABULARY
IN CONTEXT
What does **exercise** mean? Highlight details that help you understand the meaning of the word. Use the picture too.

A blizzard action plan will keep you safe.

Develop Vocabulary

Write

strong	tornado	blizzard	powerful

It snows during a ______________________.

It is windy during a ______________________.

Directions Read aloud the vocabulary words and the sentences to students. Have them choose the word that best completes each sentence and write it on the lines.

Check for Understanding

Write

1. What are these texts about?

2. Why does the author use numbers in the text?

3. Why do you think it is important to pack a flashlight?

Directions Read the questions aloud, one at a time, and have students write their responses. Remind them to use text evidence.

Compare and Contrast Texts

When we **compare and contrast** texts, we tell how they are alike and different.

Draw

Tornado Action Plan

Blizzard Action Plan

Directions Read the headings on the Venn diagram aloud. Have students draw one way the ideas in *Tornado Action Plan* and *Blizzard Action Plan* are alike in the center section. Then have them draw one way the ideas in the texts are different in each outside circle. Remind students to go back to what they underlined in the texts.

Ask and Answer Questions

We can **ask and answer questions** to get information and better understand a text.

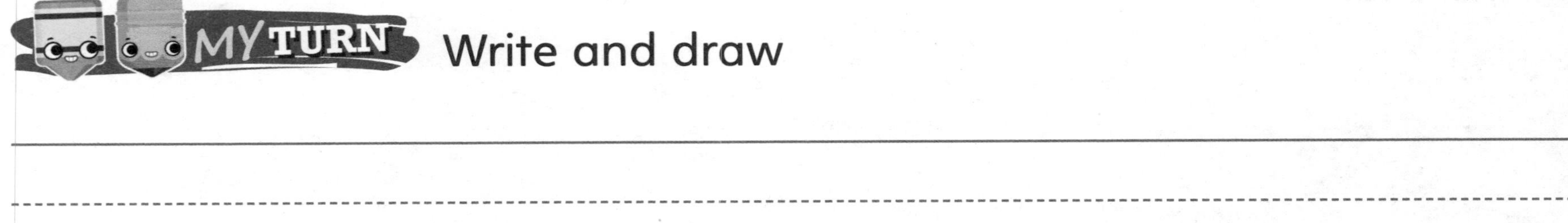

Write and draw

Directions Read the information aloud. Then have them dictate or write a question they had about the text during reading or a new question they ask about the text. Prompt them to look back at what they highlighted. Then have students use text evidence to draw a picture to answer their question.

Reflect and Share

TURN and TALK Tell your partner the steps you should follow to prepare for and keep safe in a tornado and a blizzard.

Weekly Question

How can we protect ourselves in bad weather?

Directions Tell students they read two texts about preparing for and keeping safe in bad weather. Have students respond to sources by retelling the texts. Remind them to tell the most important details from each text.

I can use words to tell about informational text.

My Learning Goal

Academic Vocabulary

effect	measure	prepare	extreme

Match

prepared

unprepared

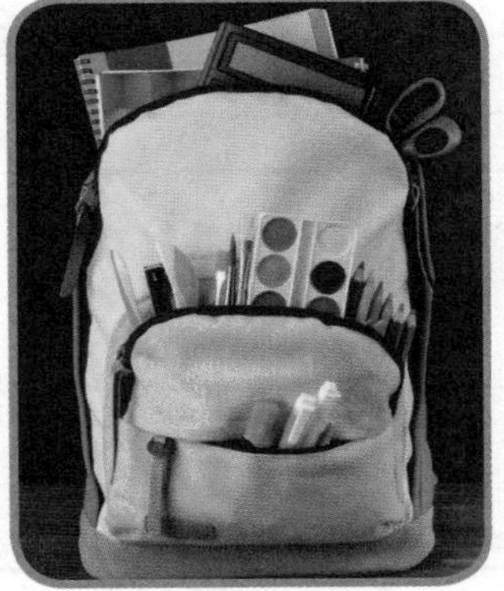

Directions Remind students that word parts can change the meanings of words. Say: The word part *un-* means "not." Have students use what they know about the meaning of the word *prepare* and the word part *un-* to match each word with the correct picture.

Spell Words

Sort and spell

swim	out	so
skip	step	spot

swim

Directions Say: Some words begin with a consonant blend. A consonant blend is two or more consonants that come together in a word, but each sound is heard. Have students determine if each word in the word bank follows the CCVC pattern. Then have them spell and write the CCVC words in the left column and the high-frequency words in the right column.

Read Like a Writer, Write for a Reader

Write

1. How are the structures of the two texts alike?

2. What is another way an author could help readers understand the order of steps?

Directions Remind students that text structure is how an author organizes a text. Have them discuss the structure of each text and how the structure contributes to the author's purpose. Then read the questions and have students write their responses.

Expand Sentences

You can **expand** sentences by adding adjectives.

Look at the wind.

Look at the **swirling** wind.

Add other words to the sentence.

Write

The snow falls.

Directions Read the information aloud and remind students that an adjective is a word that describes something. Have them think of other ways they can expand the sentence. Then read the sentence about snow aloud and have students edit it by adding an adjective. Have them write the new sentence on the lines.

I can write a nonfiction text.

My Learning Goal

Edit for Verbs

A **verb** is an action word.

Verbs can tell about actions in the past, present, or future.

Circle

I walked with Aunt Rose.

We ____________________ about school.

talk	talked

Directions Say: When you write a nonfiction text, your verbs should match. For example, they should all tell about now or all tell about the past. Read the sentences and have students edit the second sentence by circling the verb that matches the verb in the first sentence. Ask students to edit for verbs in their question and answer books.

Digital Tools Authors Use

Authors can use computers and other digital tools to write.

Circle

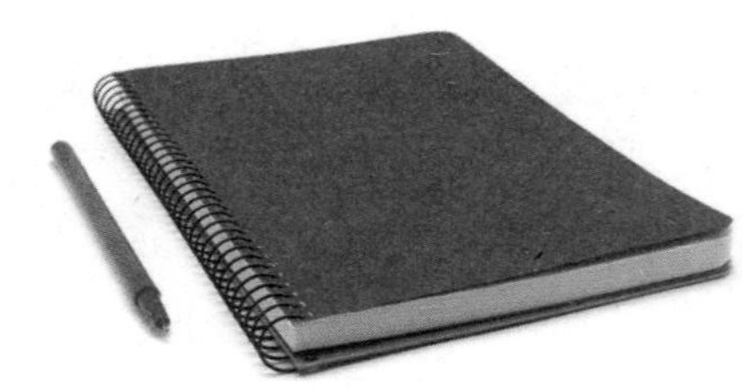

TURN and TALK Talk about how you can use these digital tools to help you write.

Directions Have students look at the pictures and circle the digital tools. Then have them talk with a partner about how they can use digital tools to write their question and answer books.

Digital Tools Authors Use

Authors can use digital tools to publish their writing.

Write

- Print the finished book.
- ______________________________.
- ______________________________.

Directions Read the first item on the list. Then have students participate in a class discussion about other ways they can use technology to publish their question and answer books, including ways they can publish the books on their own and in collaboration with peers. Ask them to write two of their ideas on the lines.

How Rain Helps Elephants

Many elephants live in hot places.

Rain makes streams and puddles.
Now this elephant has water to drink!

Rain also makes mud.
Mud helps elephants keep cool on hot days.

Weekly Question

How can rainy weather help Earth?

Draw

Directions Read the text as students look at the pictures. Ask them to discuss how rain helps elephants live in hot places. Have students interact with the source by illustrating one way rain helps elephants.

Words for Ll, Nn

Tim can go to the lake.

She must not be late.

Who will go next?

Directions Remind students that *l* makes the sound /l/ and *n* makes the sound /n/. Have students read the sentences. Ask them to circle the words with the letter *l* and underline the words with the letter *n*.

Words for Rr, Zz

Read and write

The pad is _ed.

red

I can _ip it.

She will _un.

Directions Ask students to read each sentence and use the picture to help them complete the sentence. Then have them write the word that completes the sentence on the lines.

Words for Ll, Nn, Rr, Zz

Read

Can you zip it up?

I can help rake.

Lin is on the rug.

Zac will run a lap.

Directions Remind students that *l* makes the sound /l/, *n* makes the sound /n/, *r* makes the sound /r/, and *z* makes the sound /z/. Have partners take turns reading the sentences.

My Words to Know

new	too	when

My Sentences to Read

When can we go out?

I have a new hat!

You have a hat too.

Directions Say: There are some words we have to remember and practice. Listen as I read these words: *new, too, when*. Have students read the high-frequency words. Then have them read the sentences and underline the high-frequency words in the sentences.

Going Out

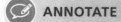

AUDIO

Audio with Highlighting

ANNOTATE

Zak had a new vest.

He could zip it up.

He set on a red hat.

Underline the words with the letter **z**.

Dad said, "We have to go."

Zak did not want to be late!

It was wet when they came out.

Look out! Do not slip!

Highlight the words with the **n** sound.

Lil came out too.

"Come ride with us," said Dad.

They all got in.

Sentences I Can Read

Read and write

- ☒ Zak rode down the lane.
- ☐ Zak rode down the lake.

- ☐ Nan has a new rate.
- ☐ Nan has a new rake.

- ☐ It is in the nest.
- ☐ It is in the next.

Directions Have students read each pair of sentences and identify which one tells about the picture. Ask them to write an X in the box by the correct sentence.

Sentences I Can Read

Read and write

zig	run	left

Max will ___run___ home.

He can go ________.

He can ________ and zag.

Directions Ask students to read the words and sentences. Then have them write the words to complete the sentences. Finally, have students read the completed sentences.

My Learning Goal I can read about weather.

Drama

A **drama**, or play, is a story that we act out for others.

Plays have characters, settings, and events.

The lines name characters and tell what they say.

Characters

Stella: Look! It is snowing!

Jason: What should we do?

Stella: Let's make a snowman!

TURN and TALK How is the play different from an informational text about snow?

Directions Read the genre information and model text aloud. Ask them to discuss the main characters in the play and tell how they know who is speaking each line. Then have partners talk about how this play about the weather is different from an informational text about weather.

Drama Anchor Chart

Main Characters

Who Likes Rain?

Preview Vocabulary

rain	dirt	seeds

Read

Read the text and look at the pictures to learn why rain is important.

Meet the Author

Stephen Krensky has written more than one hundred children's books, including board books, chapter books, and almost everything in between.

Read Together

Genre Drama

Who Likes Rain?

written by Stephen Krensky  illustrated by Carolina Farias

Characters:

 Jenna

 Frank

 Mom

AUDIO

Audio with Highlighting

 ANNOTATE

 I want to play.

 I want to play too.

CLOSE READD

Underline one thing that Frank says.

I can get there first.

No, I can get there first.

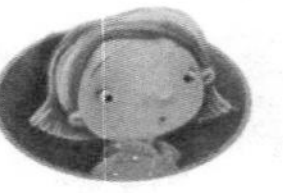 It's raining! We cannot play.

How do Frank and Jenna feel about rain? Highlight the words that tell how they feel.

 I don't like rain.

 I don't like rain, either.

 Why don't you like rain? Rain is good.

Rain makes the dirt wet.
Rain makes the seeds
wet under the dirt.
Rain helps the seeds grow into trees.

Underline one thing that Jenna says.

 No rain would mean no trees.

 No trees?

 No treehouses?

 I like rain.

 I like rain too.

CLOSE READ 

How do Frank and Jenna feel about rain at the end of the play? Highlight the words that tell how they feel.

 I'm thirsty.

 I'm thirsty too.

 Trees are not the only things that need water!

Develop Vocabulary

rain

dirt

seeds

Directions Read the words aloud. Ask them to circle the picture that shows the meaning of each word.

Check for Understanding

Write

1. How is a play different from other stories?

2. Why does the author show faces by the text?

3. How are Frank and Jenna alike?

Directions Read aloud the questions and have students write their responses. When they are finished, ask students to discuss how the main characters are alike using their responses to question 3.

Discuss Characters in Drama

A play has **main characters.**

The main characters are who the play is mostly about.

MY TURN Write and draw

Directions Read aloud the information and discuss the main characters in the play with students. Have them tell what they learned about the characters. Then ask students to choose a character, write the character's name on the lines, and draw details about the character.

Create New Understandings

Draw

Directions Say: You can use details you learn in a play to understand something new. Have students synthesize information by drawing pictures that show how Frank and Jenna feel about rain at the beginning and at the end of the play. Remind them to use what they highlighted. Then ask students to discuss how Frank's and Jenna's feelings change.

Reflect and Share

TURN and TALK Retell the events in the play. Then talk about why rain is important. Use details from the play and other texts.

Remember to tell about the most important events.

Weekly Question

How can rainy weather help Earth?

Directions Have partners take turns retelling the play. Then say: You have read other texts that tell about rain. What details have you learned about why rain is important? Have students respond to sources by discussing the answer.

I can use words to make connections.

My Learning Goal

Academic Vocabulary

effect	measure	prepare	extreme

Write

COLLABORATE Write

Directions Say: I am going to give clues about a word, and you will guess the word. Listen: *I can do this with a ruler. I can do this with a thermometer. What is my word?* Have students write the word on the first set of lines. Then have partners take turns giving clues about a word and guessing a word. Have them write their partner's word on the second set of lines.

Spell Words

MY TURN Sort and spell

too	on	zip
leg	trip	when

on

Directions Say: Short *o* is often spelled *o*, short *e* is often spelled *e*, and short *i* is often spelled *i* in two- and three-letter words. Some words begin with a consonant blend, or two or more consonants that come together in a word. Have students spell and write words with the VC, CVC, or CCVC pattern in the left column and high-frequency words in the right column.

Read Like a Writer, Write for a Reader

Circle and write

1. What is the author's main purpose for writing the play?

to persuade	to entertain

2. Pretend you want to inform readers about why rain is good. How would your text be different?

Directions Remind students that an author's purpose is the reason the author writes a text. Read aloud the first question and the answer choices and have students circle the author's purpose. Discuss students' answers and why they chose them. Then read the second question and have students write their responses.

Expand Sentences

You can **expand** sentences by adding phrases.

I like rain.

I like rain **in the morning**.

Expand your partner's sentences.

MY TURN Write

We can go.

Directions Read the information to students. Ask partners to take turns saying a simple sentence and having their partner expand it by adding a word or phrase. Then read the practice sentence and have students edit it by adding a phrase. Have them write the expanded sentence on the lines.

I can write a nonfiction text.

My Learning Goal

Edit for Spelling

Good writers check that they have spelled words correctly.

MY TURN Underline and write

Wen can I walk the dog?

Circle and write

Do not go out yet! It is weet!

Directions Tell students they have learned how to spell some words, such as *when* and *walk*. Tell them they have also learned spelling patterns and rules that can help them check their spelling, such as short e spelled *e*. Have students underline or circle each misspelled word and write the correct spelling of the word on the lines. Then have them edit their narrative nonfiction texts for spelling.

Add Details

Add **details** to make your writing better.

You can use words and pictures.

Check that you have spelled words correctly.

MY TURN Write and draw

In a blizzard, ________________ snow falls.

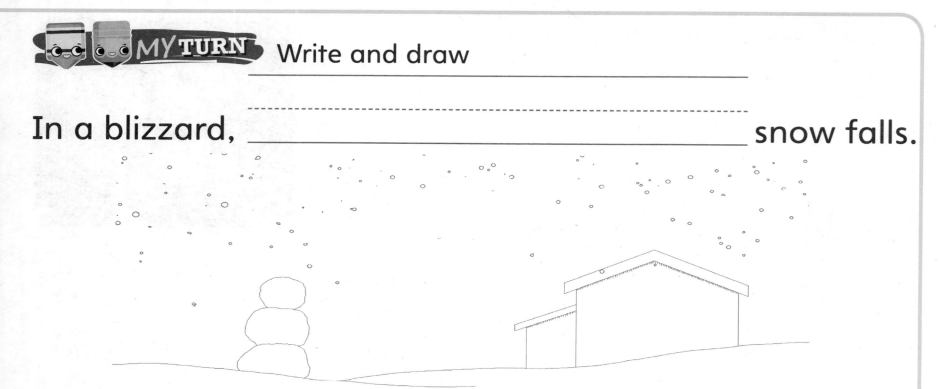

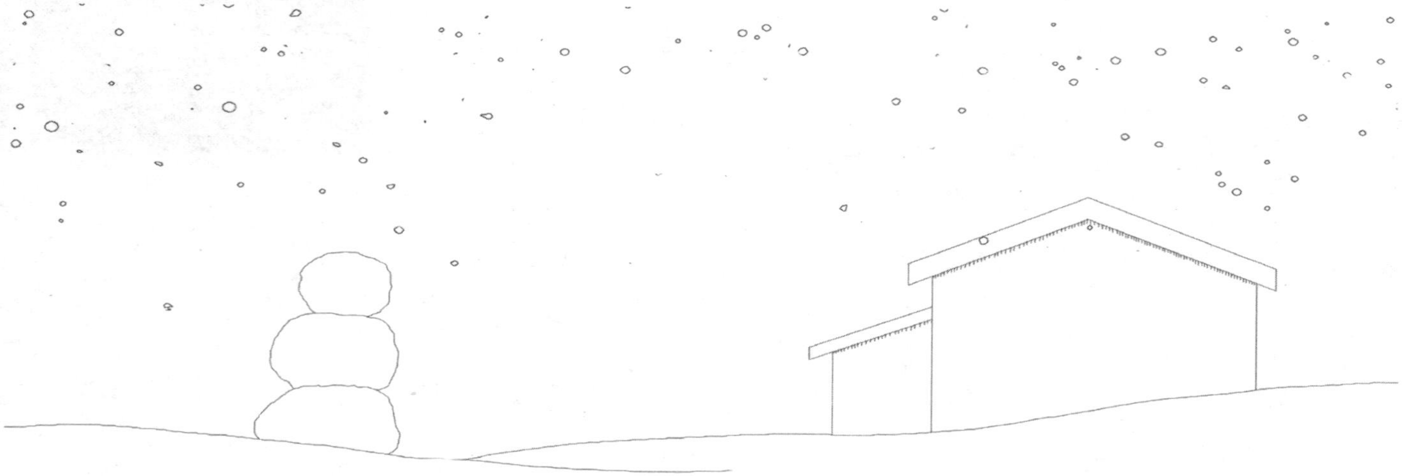

Directions Read the draft aloud and have students edit the sentence by writing an adjective on the lines. Then have them revise by adding more details to the picture of a blizzard. Say: Adding details with pictures and words makes your writing more interesting. Have students check that they have spelled words correctly.

Publish and Celebrate

Now you will share your book!

Here are some things to remember.

1. Introduce yourself and greet others.
2. Speak loudly and clearly.
3. Listen when others speak.
4. Ask questions.

TURN and TALK Practice sharing your writing with a partner. Answer questions your partner has about your writing.

Directions Read the list and discuss the items with students as necessary. Then have students work in pairs to practice introducing themselves, greeting each other, and sharing their question and answer books.

UNIT THEME

Outside My Door

TURN and TALK Go back to each text and tell one detail about weather. Use the Weekly Questions to help you.

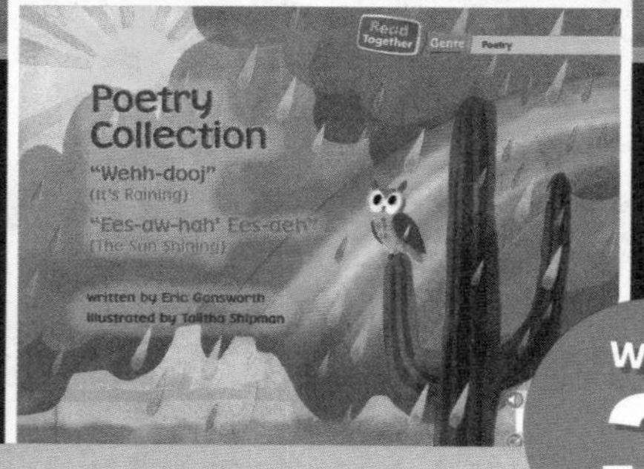

WEEK 3

Poetry Collection

How do we describe weather?

WEEK 2

A Desert in Bloom

What helps plants live in hot climates?

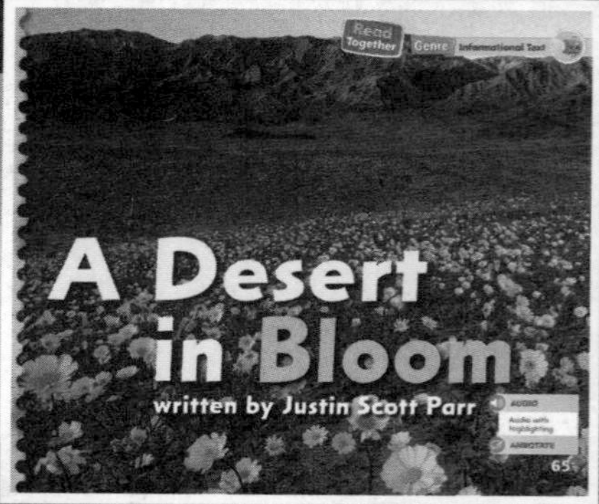

BOOK
CLUB

WEEK 1

Weather Around the World

How have people learned to live in bad weather?

Tornado Action Plan and **Blizzard Action Plan**

WEEK 4

How can we protect ourselves in bad weather?

BOOK CLUB

WEEK 5

Who Likes Rain?

How can rainy weather help Earth?

BOOK CLUB

Essential Question

What can we learn from the weather?

WEEK 6

Project

Now it is time to apply what you learned about weather in your **WEEK 6 PROJECT: The Best Weather.**

Words I Can Read

Read

it	sit	sip	lip
mad	man	van	an
job	Rob	Ron	on
up	cup	cut	nut

Directions Tell students that they can make new words by changing, adding, or deleting letters. Have partners take turns reading the words and naming the letters that were changed, added, or deleted to make new words.

Words I Can Read

Read and circle

I will ___ the bus. rid ride

The ___ is cute. cub cube

I will open the ___. not note

Directions Have students read each sentence and the answer choices. Ask them to circle the word that best completes the sentence.

Spell Words

Sort and spell

say	ox	can
sit	no	clap

ox

Directions Say: Short *a* is often spelled *a*, short *i* is often spelled *i*, and short *o* is often spelled *o* in words with two or three letters. Some words do not follow a pattern, so we have to remember how to spell them. Have students spell and write words with the VC, CVC, or CCVC pattern in the left column and the high-frequency words in the right column.

My Words to Know

no	say	under

My Sentences to Read

"Is he here?" say Mom and Dad.

No, he is not under there!

Directions Remind students that we need to remember and practice some words, such as *no*, *say*, and *under*. Have students read the high-frequency words. Then have them read the sentences and underline the high-frequency words in the sentences.

It Is Too Wet!

AUDIO

Audio with Highlighting

ANNOTATE

Look at Jude play the drum.

Look at Max play the flute.

Mom and Dad clap and smile.

Underline the words with the long **u** sound.

Jude and Max ask if they can go out.

Mom and Dad say, "No, it is too wet!"

Mom, I can go under the blue one.

Dad, I can go under the green one.

Mom and Dad say they can go.

Highlight the words with beginning blends.

Jude and Max hop and jump.

They skip and play.

It is fun to be out when it is wet!

Sentences I Can Read

Read and circle

Set it on the plate.

Please fill my glass.

Grab the blue sled.

Directions Ask students to read the first sentence. Then have them look at the pictures and circle the one that matches the sentence. Continue with the remaining sentences and pictures.

Sentences I Can Read

Read and write

can	Now	eat.	they

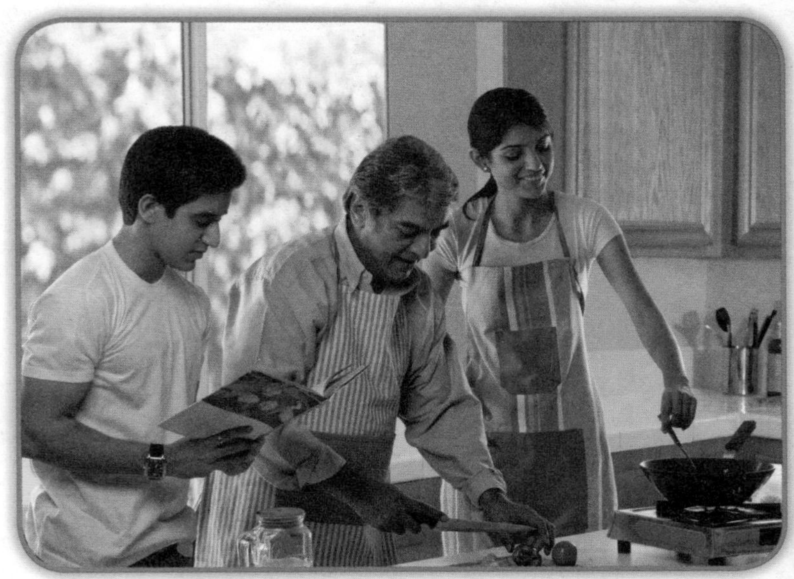

Fran will make the rice.

Rob will get some crab.

Bret will cut it up.

Directions Say: Remember that a sentence is made up of words separated by spaces. Have students read the sentences, pointing to the spaces that show where one word ends and another word begins. Then have them use the words in the word bank to write the last sentence for the story.

The Best Weather

Talk about the pictures. What type of weather do you like best?

Our favorite weather is

____

______________________________.

Directions Have students work together to talk about the types of weather in the pictures as well as other types of weather they know and discuss what type of weather they like best.

Use Words

COLLABORATE Talk to your partner about your favorite weather. Ask each other questions, such as *Why do you like it?* Use new academic words.

Weather Research Plan

Check each box as you do your project.

- [ ] Choose a type of weather.
- [ ]
- [ ]

Directions Have partners ask each other questions about their favorite type of weather. Then explain that they will write a song or poem about their favorite weather. Help students develop a research plan for the project by guiding them to write the steps on the lines.

Persuasive Poem

Persuasive texts tell an **opinion**.

They give **reasons** for the opinion.

Rainy Days

Rainy days are the best!
While we stay inside and rest,
all the plants grow green.
Everything looks new and clean!

Directions Tell students that authors write persuasive texts to convince, or persuade, readers to think or do something. Say: Poems and songs can be persuasive, or opinion, texts. Read the poem and have students tell what the author is trying to persuade readers to think or do. Ask them to circle the opinion and find and underline the reasons in the poem.

Look Online

Write

Directions Say: You can look for information about your favorite weather online. Type words that tell about the weather in a search box. Then click the magnifying glass to search. Have students work with a partner to ask questions about their favorite weather. Have them think of words they could use to search for their weather and write the words on the lines.

Take Notes

Facts About Rain

It is good for Earth.

COLLABORATE Write or draw

Directions Read aloud the research example. Say: You can get information from the title, graphics, and text of a Web site. As students research their favorite weather, have them follow the example to draw or write notes.

Add Details

Adding details makes your opinion stronger.

You can add details in pictures and other visuals.

Draw

Directions Say: Adding visuals, such as props, costumes, and pictures, can make your opinion stronger. Have students add details by drawing a picture that supports their opinion.

Share

Follow the rules for speaking and listening.

Reflect

Circle

Did I show visuals?

Did I enjoy this project?

Directions Have students review the rules for speaking and listening before performing their song or poem. Tell them to show any visuals they created. After sharing, have students reflect on their project.

Read Together

Reflect on Your Reading

Write

I liked reading about

.

Reflect on Your Writing

Write

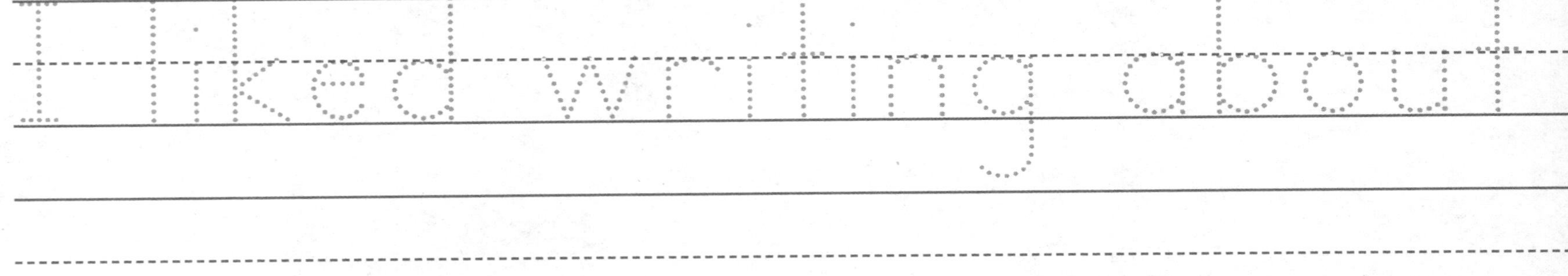

.

Directions Have students reflect on their reading and writing in this unit.

An opinion tells what you think about a topic.

I can write an opinion.

My Learning Goal

Opinion Writing

Opinion writing tells what you think or feel about a topic.

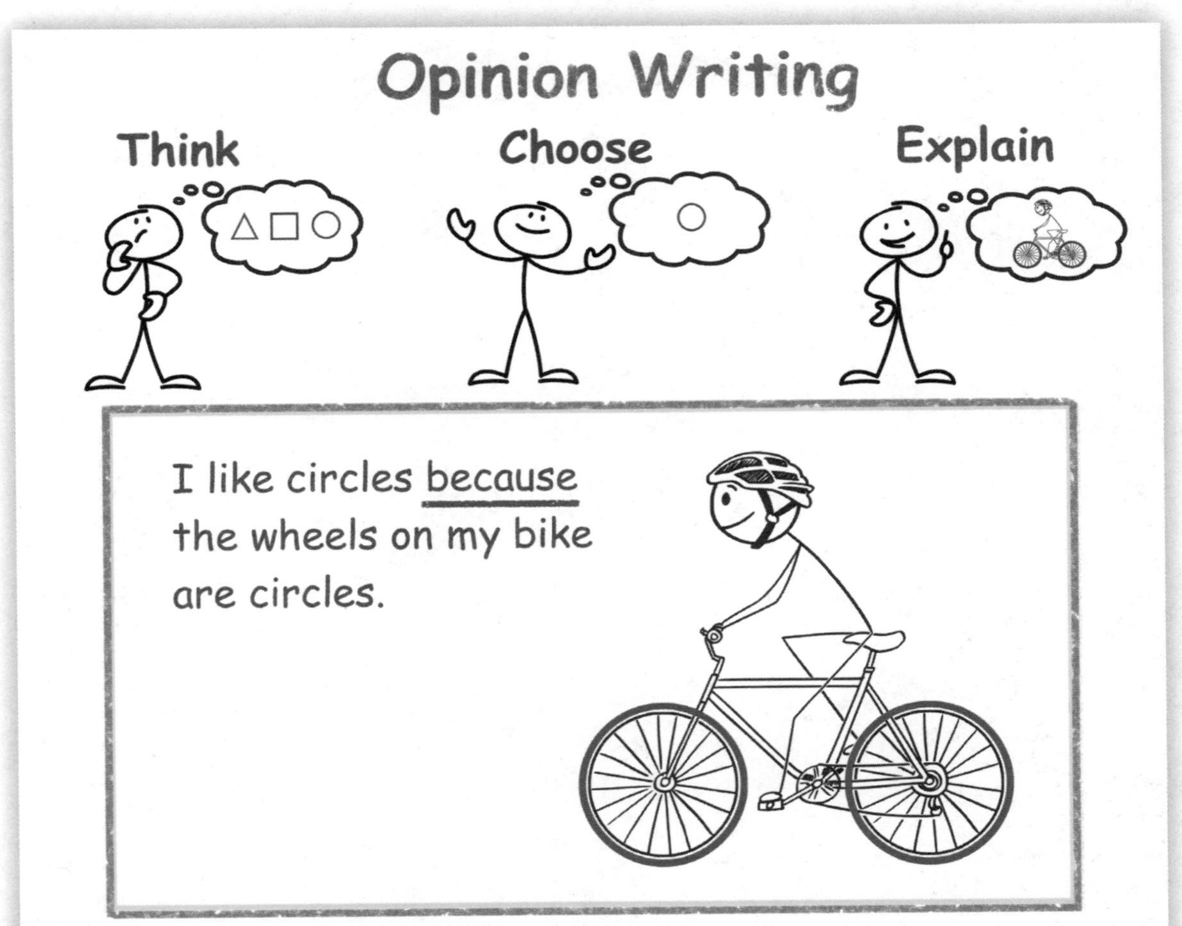

Opinion Writing
Think
Choose
Explain
I like circles because the wheels on my bike are circles.

Directions Read the text of the anchor chart to students. Discuss the characteristics of an opinion piece.

Brainstorm Ideas

An opinion is about a topic.

Draw

Directions Say: Before you write, you can plan by talking with others about a topic you might write about. Have students brainstorm ideas for writing through class discussion. After the discussion, have students draw topics that interest them.

Plan Your Opinion Writing

Authors plan what they will write about a topic.

Draw or Write

My Topic	My Choices

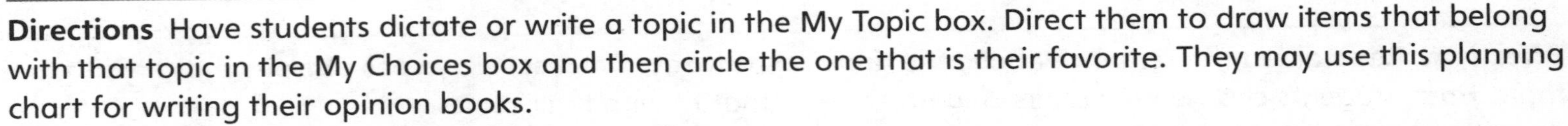
Directions Have students dictate or write a topic in the My Topic box. Direct them to draw items that belong with that topic in the My Choices box and then circle the one that is their favorite. They may use this planning chart for writing their opinion books.

My Learning Goal

I can write an opinion book.

Choose a Topic

An opinion book tells the **topic.**

Draw

There are many kinds of fruits.

Directions Read aloud the sentence above the drawing box. Say: Draw several types of fruits that fit with the topic. Have students choose new topics and draw items that fit with their topics.

State an Opinion

An opinion tells your choice. It may be your favorite item in the topic.

Draw and Write

My favorite fruit is

Directions Read the introduction to students. Read aloud the sentence starter in the drawing space. Ask students to think of the fruits they like. Have students dictate or write the name of the fruit that completes the sentence and draw that fruit in the space.

Supply a Reason

A **reason** tells why you made that choice.

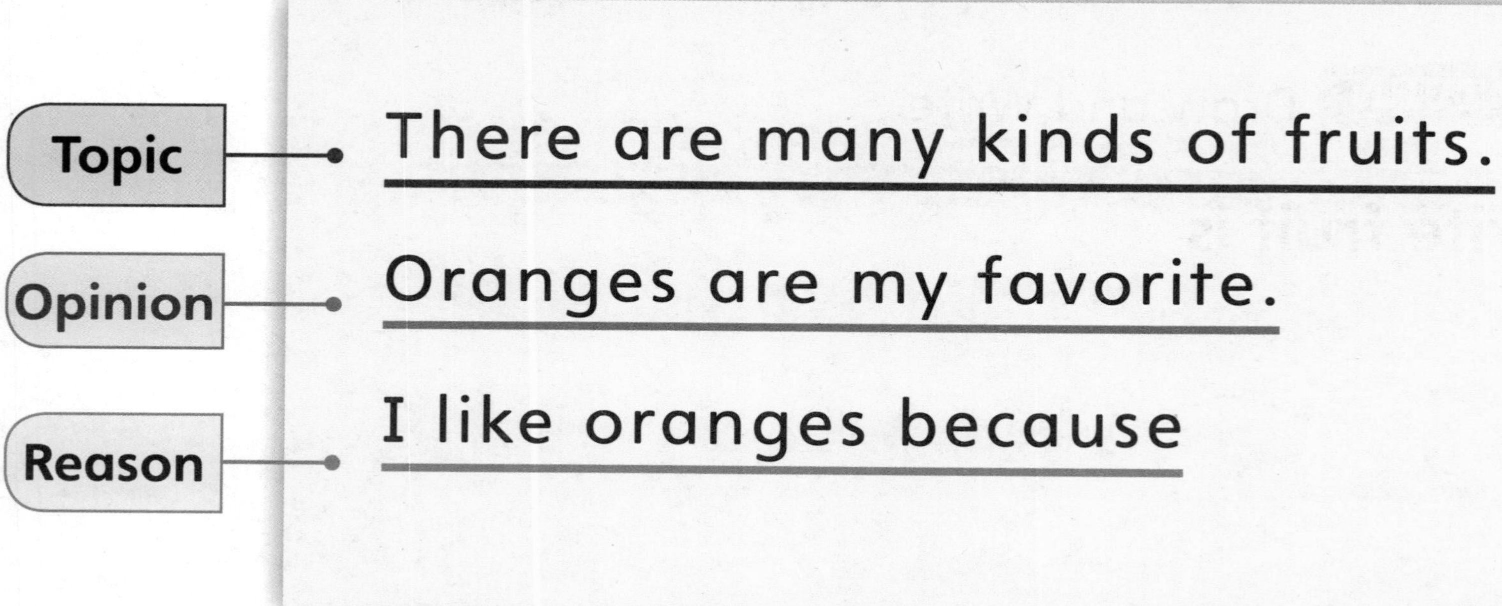

Topic
There are many kinds of fruits.
Opinion
Oranges are my favorite.
Reason
I like oranges because

Draw

Directions Read aloud the text. Have the class generate reasons why someone might choose oranges as his or her favorite fruit. Ask students to draw one of those reasons in the space provided.

I can write an opinion book.

My Learning Goal

Organize Ideas

Authors ask themselves questions before they write an opinion book.

Topic What will I write about?

Opinion Which will I choose?

Reason Why did I choose that one?

Organize the ideas for your writing.

Directions Read aloud the information and questions authors ask themselves. Model how you might answer those questions when writing an opinion book. Discuss how students will answer those questions with their own opinion books. Students may draw or write in the space provided to begin organizing ideas for their writing.

Placement of Topic and Opinion

Authors put their thoughts in order.

Topic — There are many kinds of fruits.

Opinion — Oranges are my favorite.

Reason — I like them because they taste good.

MY TURN Organize the ideas for your writing.

Directions Read aloud the information and the model text to students. Discuss how the author organized the ideas and why the ideas are organized in this way. Say: Now you can organize your own writing. Remember to dictate or write the topic, opinion, and a reason.

Placement of Drawing

Drawings help readers understand the author's opinion.

Draw

There are many kinds of fruits.

Oranges are my favorite.

I like them because they taste good.

Directions Read aloud the information and the model text to students. Discuss with the group what drawing might be helpful to include. Have students add a helpful drawing in the space provided. Say: Think about your own opinion writing. What drawing would help your readers better understand your opinion?

My Learning Goal I can write an opinion book.

Use Descriptive Words

Descriptive words tell more about a topic. Authors use descriptive words to tell how something looks, smells, feels, sounds, or tastes.

MY TURN Write

An orange tastes ______________________.

An orange feels ______________________.

I like the ______________________ smell of an orange.

Directions Read aloud the information and the incomplete sentences. Have students complete each sentence with a descriptive word. Ask students to revise their own opinion books to include descriptive words.

Conjunction *and*

The word **and** helps you put two thoughts together.

Oranges are sweet and juicy.

Oranges are used for juice and smoothies.

Oranges are yummy ______________ good for you.

Directions Read aloud the introduction to students. Have students circle the conjunction *and* in the two sentences. Discuss what thoughts were joined together. Ask students to write the missing word *and* in the final sentence. Have students revise their own opinion books to include the word *and*.

Complete Sentences

A sentence is a complete thought that makes sense. A complete sentence begins with a capital letter and ends with a punctuation mark.

Write

An orange is a ____________________.

I like oranges

____________________ all like oranges.

Directions Read aloud the information about complete sentences. Discuss that the author has not completed the sentences in the box. Talk about what is missing in each sentence and have students add what is missing.

Read Together

My Learning Goal

I can write an opinion book.

Edit for Conjunctions

Authors use conjunctions to hold thoughts together. The word **and** is a conjunction.

Write

sweet juicy yummy round

Oranges are ________________ and ________________.

Directions Read aloud the introduction. Discuss how conjunctions are used. Read aloud the descriptive words that can be used to complete the sentence. Have students choose two words to describe oranges. Ask students to read their completed sentences to partners. Talk together about how the word *and* was helpful.

Edit for Complete Sentences

Authors make sure every sentence is complete and makes sense. Sentences begin with a capital letter and end with a punctuation mark.

Write

There are many kinds of fruits

I ________ oranges best.

____ranges are good for you and they taste good.

Directions Read aloud the introduction to the class. Tell students that they need to help the author check for complete sentences and write anything that is missing. Read the sentences aloud and help students determine how they can make each sentence complete.

Assessment

Here is what you have learned to do.

- ☐ Choose a topic.
- ☐ State an opinion.
- ☐ Supply a reason.
- ☐ Add descriptive words.
- ☐ Use the conjunction **and**.
- ☐ Write complete sentences.

Directions Read aloud and discuss the checklist. Answer any questions students have about the items. You may wish to ask students what else they enjoyed most about writing their opinion books.

How to Use a Picture Dictionary

This is a picture of the word.

green

This is the word you are learning.

Draw

Directions Remind students that they can use a picture dictionary to find words. Say: The topic of this picture dictionary is **categories** such as colors, shapes, and textures. Listen as I read the words. Use the pictures to help you understand the meanings of the words. Have students identify the word *bumpy* and use it in a sentence. Then have them draw a picture that shows the meaning of the word.

Categories

Colors

orange

purple

blue

Textures

smooth

rough

bumpy

soft

Shapes

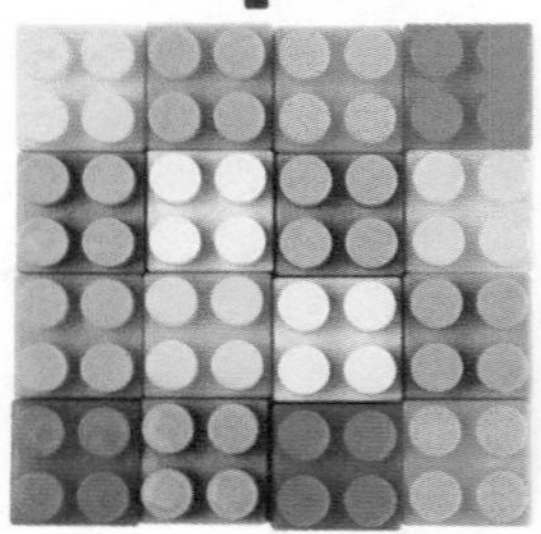

square

circle

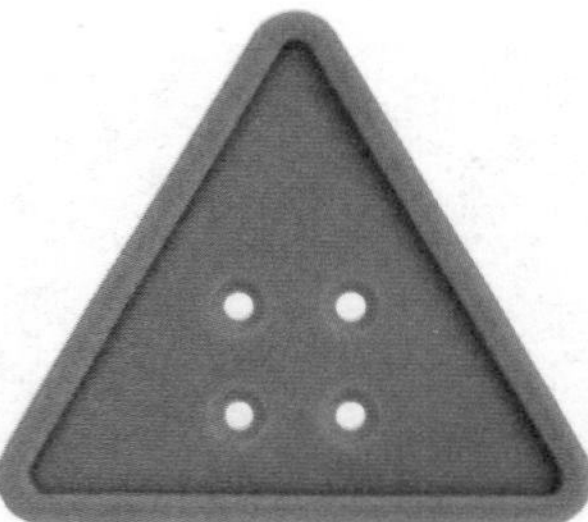

triangle

rectangle

How to Use a Glossary

The word is in dark type.

Ss **squash** A **squash** is a type of fruit that grows on a vine.

All words that begin with the letter S will be after Ss.

This sentence will help you understand what the word means.

Draw

Directions Tell students they can use a glossary to help them find the meanings of words they do not know. The words in a glossary are in alphabetical order. Have students find the word *rainy* and draw a picture to show the meaning of the word.

Bb

blizzard A **blizzard** is a storm with strong winds and blowing snow.

bloom When plants **bloom**, they open into flowers.

Dd

desert A **desert** is a dry area of land with few plants and animals.

dirt **Dirt** is another word for soil.

Ee

effect An **effect** is something that is made to happen.

extreme Something that is **extreme** is very serious or severe.

Gg

ground The **ground** is the soil or dirt on the surface of the earth.

Mm

measure When you **measure**, you find out the size or amount of something.

mound A **mound** is a small hill.

Read Together

Pp

powerful Something that is **powerful** is very strong.

prepare When you **prepare**, you get ready for something ahead of time.

Rr

rain **Rain** is the water that falls in drops from the clouds.

rainy When it is **rainy**, there is a lot of rain.

roots **Roots** are the part of plants that grow underground.

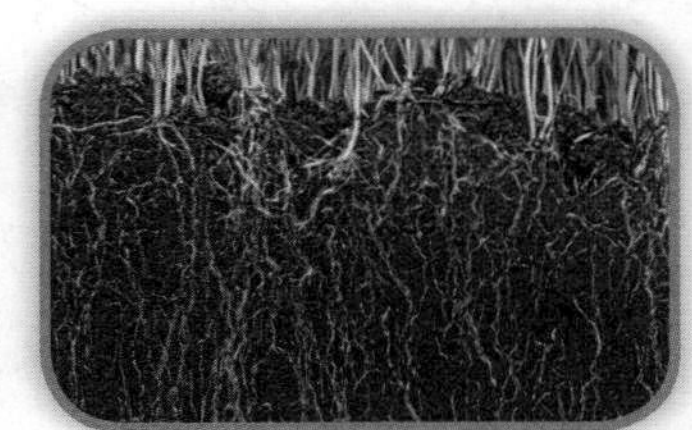

Ss

seeds **Seeds** are the part of plants that grow into a new plant.

shoots **Shoots** are the new part of plants growing out.

snow **Snow** is water that freezes high up in the air.

soil **Soil** is the loose earth in which plants grow.

squash A **squash** is a type of fruit that grows on a vine.

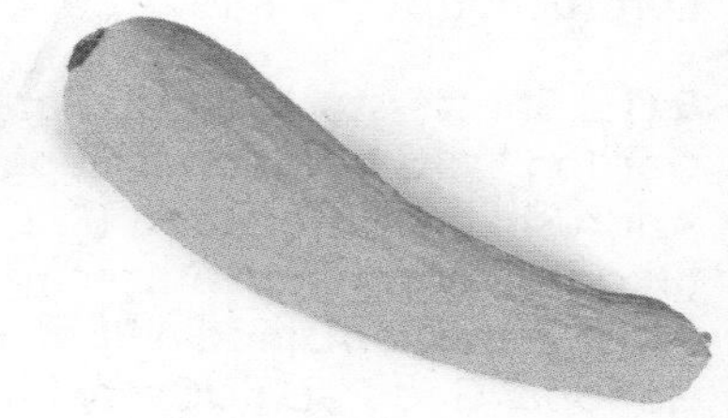

strong Something that is **strong** has a lot of force.

Tt

tornado A **tornado** is a very strong storm with wind that twists in a funnel.

Ww

weather **Weather** is what the air outside is like at a certain place and time.

windy When it is **windy**, the air is moving.

Photographs

Photo locators denoted as follows Top (T), Center (C), Bottom (B), Left (L), Right (R), Background (Bkgd)

5 (TL) Shutterstock, Satish Parashar/Dinodia Photo/AGE Fotostock, Gordon Wiltsie/National Geographic/Getty Images, Galyna Andrushko/Shutterstock, (BL) Phitha Tanpairoj/Shutterstock; **8** (Bkgd) JB Manning/Shutterstock, (BL) 123RF; **9** (TL) Shutterstock, Satish Parashar/Dinodia Photo/AGE Fotostock, Gordon Wiltsie/ National Geographic/Getty Images, Galyna Andrushko/ Shutterstock, (TCL) Phitha Tanpairoj/Shutterstock; **12** (C) 596908/ Shutterstock, (L) Piotr Tomicki/Shutterstock, (R) Creative Travel Projects/Shutterstock; **13** (BCR) Roman023 Photography/ Shutterstock, (BR) Sheri Armstrong/123RF, (TCR) Amble Design/ Shutterstock, (TR) IgorXIII/Shutterstock; **14** (Bkgd) Igor Zh./ Shutterstock, (BCL) Suti Stock Photo/Shutterstock, (BCR) Mihai Simonia/Shutterstock, (BL) Brian A. Jackson/Shutterstock, (BR) Kichigin/Shutterstock, (C) Carolina K. Smith MD/Shutterstock, (CR) Colorlife/Shutterstock; **15** Stanisic Vladimir/Shutterstock; **17** (B) VisanuPhotoshop/Shutterstock, (C) Kridsada Krataipet/ Shutterstock, (T) Petrenko Andriy/Shutterstock; **25** Africa Studio/ Shutterstock; **26** Jim Feliciano/Shutterstock; **29** (BL) 151171/ Shutterstock, (BR) Satish Parashar/Dinodia Photo/AGE Fotostock, (TL) Gordon Wiltsie/National Geographic/Getty Images, (TR) Galyna Andrushko/Shutterstock; **30** Umberto Shtanzman/Shutterstock; **31** (L) JasonDoiy/E+/Getty Images, (R) Karenfoleyphotography/ Getty Images; **32** Design Pics Inc/Alamy Stock Photo; **33** Tunart/ Getty Images; **34** Xia Yuan/Moment/Getty Images; **35** 2j architecture/Shutterstock; **36** (BL) Tunart/Getty Images, (BR) 2j architecture/Shutterstock, (C) Satish Parashar/Dinodia Photo/ AGE Fotostock, (TL) Design Pics Inc/Alamy Stock Photo, (TR) Karenfoleyphotography/Getty Images; **37** PeopleImages/E+/ Getty Images; **40** (B) Tunart/Getty Images, (T) Design Pics Inc/ Alamy Stock Photo; **43** Stockyimages/Shutterstock; **46** FamVeld/ Shutterstock; **50** JeniFoto/Shutterstock; **51** Patty Chan/ Shutterstock; **52** (B) Protasov AN/Shutterstock, (C) Dushlik/ Shutterstock, (T) Kirsanov Valeriy Vladimirovich/Shutterstock; **53** (B) Standret/Shutterstsock, (C) Hintau Aliaksei/Shutterstock, (T) Africa Studio/Shutterstock; **60** (B) Monkey Business Images/ Shutterstock, (C) Mykhaylo Palinchak/Shutterstock, (T) Rawpixel/ Shutterstock; **61** (B) Aleksey Stemmer/Shutterstock, (C) Alexey Y. Petrov/Shutterstock, (T) FamVeld/Shutterstock; **62** (C) Taro911 Photographer/Shutterstock, (L) EdgeOfReason/Shutterstock, (R) Vicki Smith/Shutterstock; **65** (C) Phitha Tanpairoj/Shutterstock, (L) Gwoeii/Shutterstock; **66** Vadimfogel/Getty Images; **67** Gianpiero Ferrari/FLPA/Science Source; **68** Lucky-photographer/ Shutterstock; **69** Keith Levit/123RF; **70** Kris Wiktor/Shutterstock; **71** (B) Sigrun Saemundsdottir/Shutterstock, (T) Pavlo Vakhrushev/ Alamy Stock Photo; **72** Morrhigan/Getty Images; **73** Ron Thomas/ E+/Getty Images; **74** (BL) Peter Gudella/Shutterstock, (BR) Wachi-w/Shutterstock, (TL) Antonfoltin/123RF, (TR) Winiki/ Shutterstock; **76** (BL) Sigrun Saemundsdottir/Shutterstock, (BR) Morrhigan/Getty Images, (TL) Keith Levit/123RF, (TR) Kris Wiktor/ Shutterstock; **79** Lucky-photographer/Shutterstock; **82** Ron Thomas/E+/Getty Images; **83** Dark Moon Pictures/Shutterstock; **84** Athapet Piruksa/Shutterstock; **86** Romrodphoto/Shutterstock; **87** Patrick Foto/Shutterstock; **88** (B) Ilike/Shutterstock, (C) Moonborne/Shutterstock, (T) Wavebreakmedia/Shutterstock; **96** (BL) Maximkabb/123RF, (BR) Dragon Images/Shutterstock, (CL) Tracy Whiteside/Shutterstock, (CR) Rawpixel/Shutterstock, (TL) Hurst Photo/Shutterstock, (TR) Nick Biebach/123RF; **100** (TCL) ND700/Shutterstock, (TCR) Elena Elisseeva/Shutterstock, (TL) Madlen/Shutterstock, (TR) ER 09/Shutterstock; **110** (BCR) ER 09/ Shutterstock, (BR) ND700/Shutterstock, (TCR) Madlen/Shutterstock, (TR) Elena Elisseeva/Shutterstock; **112** (BL) Elenamiv/Shutterstock, (CL) ND700/Shutterstock, (CR) NYS/Shutterstock, (BR) Elena Elisseeva/Shutterstock; **115** Taro911 Photographer/Shutterstock; **122** (T) Kikuchi/Shutterstock, (B) Kikuchi/Shutterstock; **123** Kikuchi/Shutterstock; **124** (B) Andrey Armyagov/123RF, (C) Wong Yu Liang/Shutterstock, (T) 123RF; **125** (B) Artmim/Shutterstock, (T) 123RF, (C) Pakowacz/Shutterstock; **132** (B) NadyaEugene/ Shutterstock, (T) Sebnem Ragiboglu/123RF; **134** (C) Andrienko Anastasiya/Shutterstock, (L) Nataliia Kravchuk/123RF, (R) Zurbagan/ Shutterstock; **157** (B) Didecs/123RF, (T) Nikola Bilic/Shutterstock; **162** (C) Nataliia K/Shutterstock, (L) Merznatalia/123RF, (R) Oleksiy Mark/Shutterstock; **164** (Bkgd) PanicAttack/Shutterstock, (BL) Dmitry Pichugin/Shutterstock, (CR) Nimmersatt/Shutterstock, (TR) Efimova Anna/Shutterstock; **165** Marius Dobilas/Shutterstock; **167** (C) Skvalval/Shutterstock, (T) Fatih Kocyildir/Shutterstock; **174** (B) Steve Byland/Shutterstock, (C) Sergey Novikov/Shutterstock, (T) Petr Bonek/Shutterstock; **175** Absolutimages/Shutterstock; **178** (L) Taro911 Photographer/Shutterstock, (C) Madlen/Shutterstock,

(R) Bouybin/Shutterstock; **188** (BL) Madllen/123RF, (BR) Bouybin/Shutterstock, (CL) Madlen/Shutterstock, (CR) Thaiview/Shutterstock, (TL) Triff/Shutterstock; **197** Dark Moon Pictures/Shutterstock; **203** (T) Stockagogo, Craig Barhorst/Shutterstock, (BR) Grandnat/Shutterstock, (C) Rosa Jay/Shutterstock; **210** (BL) Veniamin Kraskov/Shutterstock, (BR) Wk1003mike/Shutterstock, (CL) ESB Professional/Shutterstock, (CR) Africa Studio/Shutterstock, (TL) Kyselova Inna/Shutterstock, (TR) Nadiya Teslyuk/123RF; **211** Hemant Mehta/123RF; **212** (Bkgd) Rudy Lopez Photography/Shutterstock, (BR) Taiga/Shutterstock, (CL) Patchara Panchan/Shutterstock, (BCL) WDG Photo/Shutterstock, (TL) Breezeart/Shutterstock; **216** Rawpixel/Shutterstock; **236** Lotus Studio/Shutterstock; **237** (blue) Kubais/Shutterstock, (bumpy) Pan Stock/Shutterstock, (circle) Viktor1/Shutterstock, (orange) Nik Merkulov/Shutterstock, (purple) Gumenyuk Dmitriy/Shutterstock, (rectangle) Winai Tepsuttinun/Shutterstock, (rough) TSpider/Shutterstock, (smooth) Utima/123RF, (soft) Ian 2010Shutterstock, (square) Timquo/Shutterstock, (triangle) Richard Peterson/Shutterstock; **239** (B) Winiki/Shutterstock, (C) Antonfoltin/123RF, (T) Creative Travel Projects/Shutterstock; **240** (B) Madlen/Shutterstock, (T) Peter Gudella/Shutterstock; **241** (B) ER 09/Shutterstock, (T) Taro911 Photographer/Shutterstock; **242** (BCR) 151171/Shutterstock, (BR) Winiki/Shutterstock, (TCR) Elena Elisseeva/Shutterstock, (TR) Bouybin/Shutterstock; **243** ND700/Shutterstock.

Illustrations

19–23 Jok Coglitore; **27, 63, 99, 135, 214** Ken Bowser; **55–59** Juan Caminador; **91–95, 97** Laura Zarrin; **101–109, 118** Talitha Shipman; **121** Peter Benson; **127–131** Sean O'Neill; **137–151, 152, 160** André Ceolin; **169–173** Caroline Hu; **177** Chris Vallo; **179–187, 196** Carolina Farias; **198** Tim Johnson; **205–209** Nancy Poydar; **215** Rob Schuster

NOTES

NOTES

NOTES